Fast Cash

The Young Adult's Guide to Detailing Cars, Boats, & RVs

By: Jen Shulman

Foreword by: Rob Schruefer,
President of The International Detailing Association

Afterword by: P. Shawn Rowan,
Certified Body and Paint Technician and
Vice President of Sales & Global Marketing for Ardex Labs

FAST CASH: THE YOUNG ADULT'S GUIDE TO DETAILING CARS, BOATS, & RVS

1405 SW 6th Avenue • Ocala, Florida 34471 • Phone 800-814-1132 • Fax 352-622-1875
Website: www.atlantic-pub.com • Email: sales@atlantic-pub.com
SAN Number: 268-1250

Library of Congress Cataloging in Publication Control Number: 2016050057

Printed in the United States

PROJECT MANAGER AND EDITOR: Rebekah Sack • rsack@atlantic-pub.com
ASSISTANT EDITOR: Yvonne Bertovich • yvonne.bertovich34@gmail.com
INTERIOR LAYOUT AND JACKET DESIGN: Nicole Sturk • nicolejonessturk@gmail.com
COVER DESIGN: Jackie Miller • millerjackiej@gmail.com

Reduce. Reuse.
RECYCLE.

A decade ago, Atlantic Publishing signed the Green Press Initiative. These guidelines promote environmentally friendly practices, such as using recycled stock and vegetable-based inks, avoiding waste, choosing energy-efficient resources, and promoting a no-pulping policy. We now use 100-percent recycled stock on all our books. The results: in one year, switching to post-consumer recycled stock saved 24 mature trees, 5,000 gallons of water, the equivalent of the total energy used for one home in a year, and the equivalent of the greenhouse gases from one car driven for a year.

Over the years, we have adopted a number of dogs from rescues and shelters. First there was Bear and after he passed, Ginger and Scout. Now, we have Kira, another rescue. They have brought immense joy and love not just into our lives, but into the lives of all who met them.

We want you to know a portion of the profits of this book will be donated in Bear, Ginger and Scout's memory to local animal shelters, parks, conservation organizations, and other individuals and nonprofit organizations in need of assistance.

— Douglas & Sherri Brown,
President & Vice-President of Atlantic Publishing

Table of Contents

Foreword

If you would have told me 12 years ago that I would see a million dollars in revenue from cleaning cars, I would have thought you were crazy. I can tell you that it is possible, and there are people in the auto detailing industry who do it every year. Hard work, a good attitude, and some entrepreneurial spirit can make owning your own successful auto detailing business a reality.

I started my detailing company in 2004 with no capital and a $2,000 loan to purchase a van. Today, I employ 40 people, run seven mobile detailing units, operate a shop, run the detailing department for car dealerships, and established a small detailing location in a local casino's garage. I was also elected President of the International Detailing Association (IDA) and have been requested to provide seminars at various detailing trade shows throughout the year.

The past few years have seen a drastic change in the way that the public views the auto detailing profession. No longer are we seen as just car washers, but we're seen as tradesmen that are providing a skilled craft. Groups like the International Detailing Association have been leading the way to bring awareness to the public that all detailers are not the same and that you should expect a level of knowledge and professionalism from a detailer that you hire. There are now certification exams that can be taken to show your customers and yourself that you have achieved benchmarks in knowledge and practical skills. I am also seeing a growing camaraderie between detailers. What was once a battle of egos is now a chance to learn and grow from leaders in the industry. The detailing industry is changing, and this is an exciting time to be involved.

Getting started with a manual like this will be a fantastic introduction to your detailing career. There is much to learn in the beginning, and no one expects you to do it alone. You will find that the hardest part will be the transition from detailing technician to detailing business owner. It is a completely different set of skills. Not fully understanding the job of business owner is the reason that most start-up detailing companies do not survive their first year in business. Take the time to comprehend what is included in these pages as it is an important first step to the success of your business.

Once open, do not be afraid to get yourself out there to promote your business. Local networking groups, rotary clubs, and a chamber of commerce are great places to meet other local business people to let them know you exist. Lean on organizations like the IDA to stay on top of industry news and continuing education. Attend trade shows to keep up with trends in equipment, chemicals, and techniques. Tradeshows like Mobile Tech, SEMA, and DetailFest are also fantastic places to attend seminars and to have one-on-one discussions with industry leaders. Remember: there is always more to learn.

Good luck, and I hope to see you join the ranks of successful detailing business owners in our ever-growing industry.

Rob Schruefer
Owner, On The Spot Mobile Detailing
President of The International Detailing Association
Columbia, MD

Introduction

When your peers think of auto detailing, one of the first images to come to mind might be the 70s-style logo of the hit reality show *Pimp My Ride*. But you—you know that auto detailing is much more than Xzibit flashing his pearly whites and exclaiming "Yo Dawg!"

It's not just about making a car look great; half the job is knowing how to run a business and how to get (and keep) clients. Millions of people are drawn to the field as it provides accessibility, stability, and a way to establish yourself as a new business owner at a relatively low cost—not to mention it's just plain fun to hang out with cars! If you believe you have the ability to bring high shine to cars and the industry as a whole, keep reading to find out exactly how you can make your dreams a reality.

Chapter 1: Finding First Gear

Americans have had a love affair with their cars since the early 1900s when Henry Ford became a household name after he innovated the first combustion engine. As a society, we have spent our time since then rebuilding communities to accommodate our decked-out automobiles and bulldozing old buildings so we can create more parking. Sports cars, weekend cars, convertibles, collector cars, and the allure of a good road trip are just a few of the things that make the world of automobiles exciting and profitable. Yes, profitable! For every person who loves a car, there is someone else who needs to restore and detail that car, and therein lies a very lucrative market.

Fast Fact

In 1769, Nicolas-Joseph Cugnot built the first self-propelled road vehicle for the French army. It had three wheels and travelled 2.5 mph.[1]

Detailing a car is not just a simple wash and wax, and while those elements are important, there is considerably more to the job. Professionals in this

1. Library of Congress, accessed November 2016.

field also provide special services that restore vehicles to tip-top shape for showrooms or people who just really love a sparkling ride. This process can include reconditioning upholstery, removing odors, tinting windows, repairing dents, dying carpets, and much more. And since you are reading this, you probably understand the value of someone who can provide these services with enthusiasm and skill. Perhaps the world of detailing is something you have considered as a future profession, in which case you are in the right place. Soon, you will not only understand the car detailing business but more importantly, how you can make a serious living doing something enjoyable and gratifying.

Making the Scene

Despite the expense of purchase and upkeep, the American car culture is still very much alive and is always in need of qualified people to make it tick. That's where you come in. Based on extensive statistics, it's clear that people are holding on to their cars longer, perhaps for economic reasons or simply because they love their car. Either way, the older a car gets, the more important general upkeep becomes. The declining sales of new cars is good news for the detailing industry because it means people will likely put the money they have saved into fixing up one they already own. So, for you — the aspiring auto detailer — the opportunity is there for the taking. Are you ready?

The profession of detailing is nothing new, and has actually been around for decades. In the past, however, only the richest people were able to afford car detailing—until dealers in the 1940s realized a simple "spit and shine" added considerable luster and could bring in a lot of mid-range customers. This is essentially where modern car detailing began and why it continues to thrive today. Why? Because it's a practical, necessary service that will probably never become irrelevant. The demand will likely always exist, which is one of the most important factors to consider when choosing a profession.

Great, so what does it take to make it as a successful car detailer? The first thing it takes is patience—there's a lot to consider before getting started, so it's best to thoroughly educate yourself before heading off in any one direction. If you have ever painstakingly washed or waxed your own car, you already have the basic skills as a detailer. The next step will be to gain understanding of exactly what the profession entails in a broader sense.

Learn From a Pro

When in doubt, ask someone who knows what he or she is talking about. Let's take some advice from R.L. "Bud" Abraham who has been working in the car industry for more than 40 years. He has owned two franchised detailing shops in Portland, Oregon, where he became a leading manufacturer of auto detailing systems and related products. Bud occupies seats on many car detailing associations and has spent the better part of his life having great success in his industry. As a graduate of the University of Portland, he has been able to edit several trade journals and contribute to numerous online forums. He is frequently requested to speak at industry trade shows because he's simply a guy who knows his stuff.

So, when Bud says the world of detailing has room for improvement, it's best to listen to this advice. "It is still an industry using primitive technology, like heavy electric buffers, shop vacuums, chemicals in plastic bottles, rags, and buckets," he said. "There continues to be general mess and disorganization in shops, which are operated mostly by wannabe entrepreneurs with no formal training and not much business savvy."

Like most people in his industry, he wants to see this change by encouraging people who know what they are doing join the ranks—not those who are enticed by the low overhead of opening a shop, soon to realize they don't have the chops to make it work. Bud continues, "Overall, this industry has about as much savvy as a shoeshine business. It can be entered by almost anyone for a few hundred dollars, so just about anyone can start a business. That's why there are so many fatalities in the industry. It is not uncommon for people to go into and out of business in just a few months."

Although it is good news that the overhead cost is only a few hundred dollars, the bad news is, according to Bud, there's a lot of "riff-raff" in the world of car detailing. He attributes this to heavy part-time work and those who do it "on the side" as a way to make an extra buck. If you are going to do something, do it right and do it all the way, according to Bud. Without the necessary professionalism to keep the business running smoothly, it is doomed. On that note, Bud has developed what he considers to be a foolproof plan to separate you from those woeful "wannabes."

- *Is there a market?* This is a critical question, as not all locations or demographics are the same. Consider your area and objectively determine where the highest need might exist for your services.

- *How much will it cost?* Figure out up-front what the expenses will be to maintain a successful detailing business with enough operating capital to sustain your shop until it becomes profitable.

- *Where will the money come from?* Without the cash to get the business started, you don't stand a chance. It doesn't take much, but the money has to be in place to set up shop and cover the initial expenses.

- *How will you use it?* Once you have the money ready to go, you'll need to understand how to best apply it to your new endeavor.

- *How will you learn?* It's smart to take some small business classes or set up shop with another knowledgeable individual who can show you the ropes. You will need to learn first-hand how to set up and operate a shop to ensure your eventual success.

- *Do you have a plan?* Write a business plan explaining how you will set up shop, where the markets are, how you are going to get the public's business, and how you will create visibility for yourself. Again, knowledge is power.

- *What's your budget?* Ah, yes . . . the "B" word. Everyone needs a budget, especially a small business owner. Make sure you have one that clearly projects sales and the expenses you will incur while in operation.

According to Bud, there are a few other things you need to remember when it comes to the world of wash and wax, but for now, that'll do. No doubt we will stumble upon more of his excellent advice as we continue our journey toward becoming a small business owner extraordinaire.

Fast Fact

According to the Bureau of Labor Statistics, the average hourly wage for those in the automotive industry doing "other services" (as opposed to manufacturing) is around $17.86 per hour.[2]

2. As of September 2016.

Let's Hit The Road

One of the many cool things about working with cars is the accessibility of the trade. There are so many ways to get started, no matter who you are or what you currently own.

- **Be Independent**: Granted, this is the most expensive way to start because it requires purchasing a lot of materials up front. Leasing a building and outfitting it with functional equipment is just the beginning. You will need to hire employees to help you and manage the daily tasks required of a business owner. If you are detail-oriented (which of course, you are!), energetic, and very motivated, this could be a feasible option for you.

- **Go Express**: An express detailing business is a bit like a car wash in that the customer drives up and waits while you buff out the interior and exterior and provide any other special services. Express detailing only takes about 30 minutes and can be quite lucrative if cars continue to move through regularly throughout the day.

- **Stay Home:** Well, not really . . . but, yes! You will save a ton of cash on overhead if you can initially set up shop in your garage. By removing the cost of a building in the beginning stages, you will make money faster, but there are some issues to be aware of. First, be aware that you need proper water containment as stipulated by Federal and State standards, and a way for runoff to find the nearest sewer. Be sure to check any zoning restrictions in your neighborhood as well to ensure you are allowed to run a commercial enterprise there. Also, it's probably a smart idea to discuss this option first with your spouse or partner because you may never be able to park in your own garage again.

- **Join Others**: Franchises are turnkey operations that are usually ready to go right from the start. After paying the initial fee, you are entitled to use the provided business methods to develop your own business. This option cuts a lot of the initial planning and work out of the equation and can get you working under a recognizable shop name in no time.

- **Just Take Over**: Sometimes people are looking to sell their already established detailing shops to the highest bidder. This can be a great score for the right buyer and will save you a considerable amount of time and labor. But remember, be cautious when evaluating the business and make sure there aren't any drawbacks like bad location or poor reputation to consider. Many times, these obstacles can be overcome, but you'll want to know exactly what you are getting before it's too late to change your mind. Take the time to thoroughly research the business and identify some potential challenges.

- **Pick a Site**: Sometimes car washes are looking for qualified people to bring in detailing services they cannot provide. It's possible to find an arrangement with another business owner where you can offer your services in return for a workspace and regular customers. You will have to give the car wash owner a percentage of your earnings, but it may end up being worth it until you find another option.

- **Find a Dealer**: Where's the best place to find a lot of cars? A car lot, of course. Auto dealers are always in need of detailing before a sale, and you may be able to build up a steady flow of customers by working through the dealer.

- **Go Big**: If you can detail a car, you have the basics skills needed to detail a plane, a ship, or a train. Competition can be fierce for these positions, but once established, they can provide highly profitable and dependable work. After some experience in the field, commercial clients may become an attractive alternative to cars.

- **Drive Away**: Using your own vehicle may be the best way to find work in detailing, at least for a while. Mobile detail services are very popular and offer a whole new option for those looking to work without all the overhead cost. It is a great alternative to owning a building and paying employees. Depending on your community, it may be even more suitable than owning your own shop. To be mobile, you will need portable equipment and an onboard water system that can handle the job. This could put you on the road to a quick startup with minimal hassle.

Checking Out The Competition

Because starting a car detailing business is fairly easy, a lot of people are doing it. Don't let that stop you—just know what you are dealing with. By visualizing yourself in the industry, you will be able to identify the real competition.

- **Legit Detailing Shops:** The only thing that makes them more "legit" than you is that they have a roof—but they also have a lot more overhead expense. Because of this, they are likely to charge the customer more, so remember the art of undercutting the competition and keep your prices lower.

- **Mobile Detailers:** These guys have wheels and can go anywhere. Can you? Considering their mobility, they can enter any area and will likely compete with brick-and-mortar businesses, often earning up to $100,000 a year for themselves. Set yourself apart from mobile detailers by running the most professional shop possible with quality equipment and perhaps a vehicle of your own for "home visits."

- **Car Washers:** They can provide express maintenance and detail services while customers wait. We all know faster can often feel better, so it will be important to offer people a service that's worth waiting for.

- **Do It Yourselfers:** Yup, some weekend warriors like to wash their own cars. It will be your job to let them know they can't possibly do it as well as you can, so they should just enjoy their day off.

Fast Fact

According to IBISWorld, there aren't any companies that hold a dominant market share in the car wash and auto detailing industry. There are, however, almost 70,000 businesses that offer these services.[3]

3. As of August 2016.

Show Me The Money

Although we know about 15,000 independent car detailers are hard at work in the U.S., we don't know exactly what they earn. This is partly because prices vary widely according to region as well as the exact services the detailer provides. That being said, the best way to estimate your potential earnings is to think about what you could charge for detailing services.

As a professional, you should be able to make nearly $100 a day washing and waxing just two cars, easily something a one-person operation could accomplish. Given that rate, it's possible to imagine detailing at least four cars—which comes out to a pretty decent living. The more specialized your services are, the more you can charge, so it's worthwhile to expand your skills to include basic interior services as well.

On the other hand, if you could employ a few other people, you would increase your profit margin considerably and it would allow you to do way more in less time. Just remember, the wages for your employees have to stay below what you make overall, otherwise it's not worth it. It's all about math, so let's take a look at how much a one-person operation should be able to earn in one day by washing, waxing, and cleaning two to three cars vs. a business with employees handling up to eight vehicles a day.

One-person operation — Daily		
Number of Cars Detailed	Projected Earnings for wash/wax only	Projected Earnings for wash/wax/interior clean
2 per day	$100	$180
3 per day	$150	$270
8 per day	$400	$720

Based on a 260-day year (five days a week X 52 weeks), a detailer could earn:

One-person operation — Yearly		
Number of Cars Detailed	**Projected Earnings for wash/wax only**	**Projected Earnings for wash/wax/interior clean**
2 per day	$26,000	$46,800
3 per day	$39,000	$70,200
8 per day	$104,000	$187,000

Adds up pretty quick, doesn't it? And this is just an estimate based on the most basic services, so it's easy to see how charging more for SUVs and adding premium packages with engine detailing and leather repair could quickly raise your profits even more. A complete detailing job from hood to trunk can easily run up to $200 per vehicle, depending on your ZIP code.

The best way to really keep the money rolling in is not to kill yourself by manically detailing a bazillion cars a day but rather by finding a way to "upsell" customers on other services they might want, therefore increasingly their overall bill. Fast food restaurants have been doing this for years through "supersizing," and you can employ the same tactic for getting more out of your customers. Rather than settling for a simple wash, perhaps they would like the carpets done as well? It adds a fresh scent to the car. Maybe they want to keep the dashboard from fading by conditioning the leather? As long as you are genuine and enthusiastic, customers will enjoy the attention and often take you up on those increased services. In that sense, no one can really tell you what the total outcome earning is for a detailer — it's entirely up to you.

Chapter 2: Gentlemen (Ahem, and Ladies), Start Your Engines!

As an entrepreneur, making decisions is just part of what you *do*. When faced with the myriad of choices you must make as a business owner, don't shy away, but learn to embrace the challenge. You're in charge! Given that you may very well be a fledgling car detailer in the near future, one of the first decisions you must make is what services you will offer, as well as how to bundle them together to elicit the most lucrative price. Once you have made that decision, you essentially have your product and you can begin marketing.

What's Your Angle?

As a professional, you need an image. Are you someone who really likes to take time and focus on doing something thoroughly, or maybe you like to fill your day with a lot of smaller jobs that can be done quickly? You will need to identify this before establishing yourself in the biz.

The full service me

Are you going to offer a standalone business offering basic services like washing, waxing, and upholstery care? Or perhaps you would like to include some specialized elements like water spot removal and carpet dyeing? Once you head down this path, there are a lot of different options for customizing your product. Have you considered windshield chip repair or gold plating? A full service business offering this level of attention would attract customers who are looking for "the works" and willing to pay for it. Some of these customers may be car buffs who don't have time for detailing, people looking to spruce up a used car, lease customers getting ready to turn in their vehicle, or anyone just looking for a way to freshen up their driving experience. Regardless, all of these customers can mean money in your pocket—if you play your cards right.

A complete exterior detailing package includes:

- *Hand-washing the vehicle*

- *Using a clay bar to remove stubborn surface dirt and contaminants*

- *Drying the vehicle by hand*

- *Applying wax and sealants*

- *Cleaning windows and mirrors*

- *Applying tire and trim products*

A complete interior detailing package includes:

- *Vacuuming the floors and seats*

- *Shampooing or steam-cleaning the floor, seats, and floor mats*

- *Cleaning and conditioning leather and vinyl seats*

- *Cleaning and dressing hard surfaces such as the dashboard, door panels, and console*

- *Cleaning other related equipment such as vents, knobs, pedals, outlets, cubbies, drink holders, and door jams.*

- *Cleaning windows and the rearview mirror*

* Although not really interior or exterior, a complete detail can also include a thorough cleaning of the car's engine with a pressure washer to remove dirt and grease. After, you will need to dress it with water-based products to make it shine like new.

The express me

Another possibility you will want to consider is working as an express detailer who can offer many of the same services but without the wait. These folks won't be quite as concerned with the level of detailing but will be looking for a way to still keep their cars fit while only waiting 15-20 minutes. The upside is that while you make less money per job, it's feasible to accomplish quite a few in one day. So, the question is, "How do you want to spend your day?" Once you manage to land a customer looking for an express detail, what next?

An express exterior detailing package includes:

- *Washing the vehicle*

- *Drying the vehicle by hand*

- *Applying wax and sealants*

- *Cleaning windows and mirrors*

- *Applying tire and trim products*

An express interior detailing package includes:

- *Vacuuming the floors and seats*

- *Wiping leather and vinyl seats*

- *Cleaning and dressing hard surfaces such as the dashboard, door panels, and console*

- *Cleaning other related equipment such as vents, knobs, pedals, outlets, cubbies, drink holders, and door jams.*

- *Cleaning windows and the rearview mirror*

*No engine cleaning is necessary in an express detail job.

The mobile me

Although somewhat unconventional, a mobile detailing business offers some great benefits. The headaches of dealing with property and sizeable overhead can sometimes feel too burdensome, in which case this is smart alternative. You can service cars anywhere, at any time, and this give you freedom . . . and freedom is good. But with freedom also comes a certain responsibility to be motivated and maintain high visibility. And remember, things like weather and your own vehicle maintenance may require specific attention, so stay aware of your unique challenges.

- *Erect* a temporary canopy over your workspace if you live in inclement zone.

- *Create* services you can do when the weather is foul like putting together marketing materials.

- *Find* work in places that have shelter like limousine shops, small aircraft hangers, or boat houses.

- *Think* outside the box and be creative; when business is slow you could restore lawn furniture, recondition garage floors, or clean and sanitize dog kneels when it's cold. When it's warmer, use your pressure washer to power-clean decks, patios, and aluminum siding.

- *Learn* about the usefulness of a power-washer. These things can be used on all sorts of equipment and are essential to a mobile business. As one expert said, "I will power-wash anything. Sometimes the customer wants me to detail and then do the driveway, too. I also have a unit I use to strip stain and clean fences, and that brings me a lot of extra work. Ever since I bought a hot water unit, I've gotten extra jobs just with this piece of equipment."

The creative me

Maybe you are someone who always orders the combo plate, in which case you may want a bit of each. It's entirely possible to own a shop and provide mobile services to those who want them, in addition to offering weekend express detailing. You can also bundle your services to attract more customers, offering them a quick sense of what they need. See? Lots of options.

The specialized me

In any market, there is always room for specialization, and many customers will specifically seek out this kind of treatment for their special cars. What are some of the services you can offer that will really set you apart from the rest and identify you as a unique detailer? Some of them will require a little extra "know-how" but are entirely manageable and often very popular for car aficionados.

- *Black plastic trim restoration:* restoring the luster to exterior plastic, rubber, or vinyl parts

- *Carpet and upholstery repair and dye*: fixing damage such as burns, tears, scuffs, and fading

- *Custom paint touch-up*: filling in scratches, chips, dings, and other road damage with custom-mixed paint to match the vehicle's' original paint job.

- *Convertible and ragtop repair:* replacing motor, worn-out frame parts, and deteriorating stitching—repairing frayed and worn out spots

- *Headlight renewal*: removing yellow discoloration and eliminating fogginess

- *Overspray treatment removal*: fixing damage from road particles, chemical fallout, environmental pollutants, dust, or anything that has affected the integrity of the exterior

- *Ozone odor elimination:* using an ozone generator to remove pesky odors from pets, food, mold, mildew, smoke, or other unwanted scents

- *Paint-less dent repair:* removing small dents and dings from exterior

- *After-market coating applications:* restoring the exterior's shiny, new appearance through reapplying a clear coat

- *Guarding interior*: applying a sealant on upholstery to prevent soiling and repel water and stains

- *Sealing exterior:* covering outside of vehicle with a sealant to guard against rust, oxidation, and other contaminants

- *Trim and instrumentation repair:* replacing or fixing the knobs and trim damaged through regular use

- *Trunk detailing:* vacuuming and shampooing to remove dirt, grime, and odors

- *Undercarriage detailing:* removing all traces of undercoating, sanding rough spots, and refinishing with special conditioner

- *Windshield repair:* addressing initial chips and cracks

- *Windshield tinting:* shielding out damaging rays that can discolor upholstery

Fast Fact

Charles Edgar Duryea and his brother Frank started the first successful gas powered car in 1893. It had a 4-horsepower engine.[4]

Fair Pay

Although we all want to get paid, it's important to set your prices in a fair and equitable way that doesn't necessarily gouge the customer. The last thing you want is to be labeled as the shop that overcharges; however, you definitely don't want to undercut yourself. Before setting your fees, do a quick internet survey on what other professionals in your area are charging for their services. A full detailing service takes about 3-4 hours, so make sure you are getting paid for your time.

4. Library of Congress, accessed November 2016.

Remember Bud? Well, he has some advice on the subject that makes a lot of sense. While it's important to check out prices around you, the most sensible thing to do is assess the overall cost of the labor and expenses for one hour of work. Then consider how long it will take to complete the job and multiply your magic number with the hours needed. By doing this, you will arrive at a fairly reliable price for the service you are providing; then crosscheck your number with the competition and see where you land. According to Bud, the best way to tweak a system is to improve the "turn-rate" and try to accomplish more in less time. That will add about 20 percent to the bottom-line figure of profit and help you reach the number you need.

Who's Answering the Phone?

Oh yeah, owning a detailing business is not all about detailing—there are some other pretty important jobs that need to be addressed. Although stocking yourself with power tools and high-end products is fun, it's important to remember that, as the owner, you have other things on your plate. So, once the car is shining like new, what else needs to be handled?

- Answering the phone

- Opening the mail / Checking email

- Talking to vendors

- Calling back customers

- Purchasing supplies and products

- Updating / Managing website and online presence

- Invoicing clients

- Making payroll

- Balancing the books

- Addressing the need for advertisement

- Networking with other professionals and important contacts

- Scheduling employees

- Training workers

- Mediating employee issues

- Hiring / Firing

- Greeting customers

- Running the register and answer questions

- Making future appointments

- Banking

- Cleaning shop

- Stocking shelves

- Inventory

Now don't panic—this may seem like a lot of work, but it's all very manageable, especially if you have a few people to help you. What's important is to stay motivated and ready to take on whatever challenges might pop up from day to day. Buffing out a car in the sunshine might sound a lot more alluring than sitting in a stuffy office doing paperwork, but being self-employed requires you keep a handle on all tasks, even the ones you dislike. This is not a hobby, it's your livelihood, so be self-sufficient and remember to mentor your employees with strong leadership and a positive outlook.

Chapter 3: Creating a "Front-View Mirror"

N ow that you know what it takes to enter the world of auto detailing, the next question is how will you get people to use your services? Obviously, you can't have one without the other. When you get behind the driver's seat of a car, you need to know where you are going, right? Well, maybe it's a joyride, but you get the point—direction is key when you actually need to get somewhere. Similarly, you need to identify who your potential customers are before spending money on target advertising to reach them. In fact, you will need to spend some time thinking about how you can package yourself, your services, your business, and all that you offer into a neat brand that appeals to the public and brings in customers. The relationship sounds simple—you provide, they buy—but there are several components to bear in mind while finding this symbiosis.

Use Market Research

There are two aspects to this important step. First, use the information around you to strengthen your goals. You can determine what potential customers likely want from your business by looking around at what has already been done and its level of success. Learn from the competition. Second, think about if your services are needed in the market. Just because you really want to detail cars in a certain area does not necessarily make it a feasible choice. A smart entrepreneur understands this is only part of the decision-making process. You can offer the world's most sparkling detail, but if there's no one in your area who's willing to pay for that service, your efforts are pointless. You don't want to open a business selling ice to an Eskimo, so make sure you understand your market.

Fast Fact

The car wash and auto detailing industry generated $10 billion in revenue per year.[5]

Just as there can be too little demand in the market, there can also be over-saturation where the scene has already been flooded with similar businesses. If you can't see an original niche for yourself, you may want to consider moving on to a different location where the market is more open. Find an area where you can really shine as a business, providing a service that people in the area need, want, and can afford. This is a recipe for financial success.

Remember, this type of initial research should be your first step in starting up your business. There's no point in dumping a bunch of cash into something that isn't set up for success. Hold off on investing in any equipment, leasing a building, or stocking up on any products until you have a sense of whether the location, economy, and demographic can support your endeavor. This is called looking before you leap.

5. IBISWorld, 2016.

See The People

Although it may sound relatively dull, knowing your demographic is crucial to your success. Thanks to the internet, it's also pretty easy to do and costs nothing. Using the specifics of the area you would like to work in, do some targeted searches to uncover community profile or statistics of the neighborhoods. *What's the average income? Do people typically drive more than they take public transportation? Do people generally own or rent their homes? What are some other businesses in the area (if any) that offer the same services? How successful have they been?* You may want to peruse the Census Bureau's website and read up the demographics of your desired area. Your findings will be a reliable indication of whether your future business can succeed in that particular market, but what exactly should you look for?

- *Age*: Studies suggest more than half of full-service carwash customers are over the age of 50, so it would make sense to find a location where this demographic is well represented.

- *Gender*: Apparently, women tend to be more frequent users of detail services. Is the neighborhood you're scoping out filled with lots of soccer moms?

- *Income*: In general, can people afford your services? The higher the disposable income, the more likely a person is to frequent your business.

- *Occupation*: Again, understanding what people do for a living can translate a great deal about their income and free time. Are they busy professionals who have money to spend but with little time to detail their own car?

- *Education*: Typically the higher the education, the higher the income, so keep this in mind when conducting your market research.

Study Others

If you want to thrive, you need to understand the competition around you. Don't feel threatened or intimidated by it, just look at it with the intention of making your own business stronger. Start by assessing your direct competition, which includes not only detailing shops, but mobile outfits and car washes in the area. Even though not all car washes offer detailing, they will be pulling from the same customer base.

Check out the web pages and online reviews of other shops and get to know their strengths and weaknesses so you can build a better model for your own business. Maybe they don't work on Sundays, a day when a lot of people have free time to detail. It might be smart for you to offer hours that day. Find a way to fill the voids of the competition as well as set yourself apart.

Create a Marketing Plan

As they say, knowledge is power. Once you have armed yourself with the pertinent details of your area, you are ready to put together a successful marketing plan. This is done through simply writing down all that you have found in an organized way. It does not have to be long or heavily detailed, but it does need to include your strategy for entering the market and remaining visible to the public. Your marketing plan should discuss the following elements:

- Demographics, opportunities, services, and any other relevant information

- Prospective customers and their general profile

- Pricing strategies and how to be competitive in your market

- Marketing strategies that reflect your findings and a realistic timeline for implementation

- Financial objections you hope to reach in your first year of business

Envision Your Future

If you are truly planning to enter the profession of car detailing, you have likely already closed your eyes a few times and envisioned what your business would look like. This is comforting and an important part of the motivational planning process.

Maybe you imagine yourself talking with customers and watching them smile appreciatively at the shine on their car, or perhaps you see yourself owning a detailing superstore with an attached casino and raw bar—a place where you can become a fixture in the community. Maybe you envision being more hands-off, sitting back with you feet up while conceptually directing a chain of successful shops. No matter what your ideal situation is, it's always good to have dreams. The more you evaluate them, the more likely they will become your reality.

If you haven't already, create a vision for your business. What do you see? What do you want? Maybe your biggest goal is to become the number one detailer in your area, flying high above the rest. It may feel like wishful thinking—especially if you are just starting out on a shoestring budget—but remember, if you can imagine it, you can achieve it. Dreams are not just child's play; they are roads to a new reality.

Define Your Intent

There's one more important piece in the process of visualizing your future—your mission. Consider writing a statement for your business that defines your purpose. This can define the scope of your overall mission as a detailer and serve as a benchmark for measuring any future progress. Someday, when you are looking back as a successful business owner, your mission statement should sound like reality. Starting off, it can be a mini road map of your intentions and a way to visualize your progress. It doesn't have to be long, complicated, or lofty—just clear and manageable. For example, here's a mission statement that focuses on specialty work:

> *"To provide the best possible service to families
> and gearheads alike in the San Francisco area,
> with a focus on basic services. Specialties
> include the maintenance services necessary for
> a vehicle to survive a wet Northern California
> winter, as well as the cosmetic services that
> improve cars and make their owners proud."*

Another example would be this longer statement focusing on growth:

> *"Washing and waxing all types of vehicles will*
> *be the purpose of Lou's Details, a one-person*
> *detailing business catering to busy professionals*
> *looking for free pickup and delivery service.*
> *Initially, Lou's will detail a few cars a day;*
> *however, by the end of the year, the business*
> *will add an employee and take on more customers.*
> *This growth will occur through*
> *increasingly visibility in the community*
> *and building a loyal customer base."*

A mission statement can be as simple or as detailed as you wish, and you don't need to pay a lot of money to have someone write it. Just come up with the basic *"Who, What, Where, When, Why, and How?"* and you will be well on your way to a focused idea.

Chapter 4: When the Rubber Meets the Road

We have cleaned the car, consulted the map, and now it's time to start driving. At this point, you know what a detailer does and how to locate customers. This thing is happening, so what's next? Making it all legit and legal, that's what. You'll need to select a business name and find professionals who can help guide you on this journey.

There are four legal forms of ownership available for small business owners, and you will need to consider which one is right for you. This is best handled by consulting an attorney who specializes in commercial law or an accountant who understand small business practices. They will be able to give you sound, practical advice on how to select one of these forms of ownership.

Sole Proprietorship

Simply put, this is the easiest and most inexpensive option when forming a business. You can begin work right away and just file an extra form at tax time indicating your new business status. Depending on your state and local ordinances, however, you may also need a business license. But that's basically it. You own and manage the business and reap the profits. With that comes being personally responsible for whatever happens within that business, including debts and liabilities. The buck stops with you. This can be an empowering feeling, but it can also open you up to lawsuits if you do something thoughtless like use the wrong wax on someone's prized Bugatti or fail to create a safe work environment for your employees. Oil and water are slippery, you know.

While it's important not to dwell on the negative, just remember to be vigilant when running your own shop. If you feel comfortable assuming this risk and protecting yourself with insurance, a sole proprietorship could be ideal for you. Remember, if you are planning to raise money in the initial stages of your development, you may want to avoid this option, as banks and investors rarely want to engage with sole proprietorship businesses.

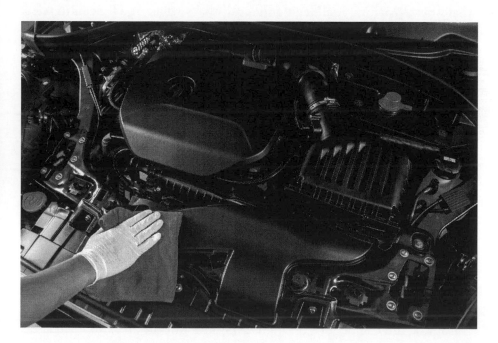

Partnership

This happens when two or more people share the ownership and assets of the business, as well as the debts and liabilities. You're all in it together. All plays in the business must report the business on their personal tax returns. That said, there are two types of partnerships to be aware of when considering such an arrangement.

- *General partnership:* This is the most common relationship and is especially effective for people who have different skills that work well together. For example, you may be adept at making cars shine like new while your partner has a head for numbers.

- *Limited partnership*: This arrangement is appropriate for partners who don't require equal standing in the business. One person would likely be the lead owner with a larger stake, while the other would contribute on a smaller scale and therefore take in proportionately less profit.

Partnerships are helpful because they allow you to share insight, knowledge, and responsibility for the business. It gives you someone to lean on in times of trouble and someone to celebrate with in times of success. However, forming a business with another person has inherent risk, even if you know the person well. Inevitably, there will be disagreements and potential problems, so choose your partner(s) wisely. To ensure a productive relationship, have a lawyer draw up articles of partnership before you launch the business. That way, if the situation doesn't work out, you have a clear plan for how to handle the next step.

Corporation

The main advantage of making your business a corporation is to legally separate yourself from it. This status limits the owner's responsibility when it comes to debt, lawsuits, or other legal problems. It is a feasible way to lower personal risk, and financial lenders are more apt to do business with you if you're incorporated. There are two types of corporations to consider:

1. *C Corporation*: This is the more standard type of corporation that offers owners and their stockholders benefits such as limited personal liability, the chance to deduct business expenses, and offer employees tax-free insurance benefits. But like with most things tax-related, there's a catch. Profits from C corporations are subject to double taxation which means owners must pay both federal and state taxes on any money they make throughout the year.

2. *S Corporation*: This is an attractive option for small business owners because it does not require the company to pay federal income tax. Instead, business profits are reported as regular income on the owner's personal tax return, which makes the overall payment to Uncle Sam considerably lower. Flip side? When the government takes less, they want more. S corporations face tougher regulations and restrictions, including mandatory citizenship.

Regardless of their differences, state governments require both types of corporations to file articles of incorporation, elect company officers and/or a board of directors, and hold an annual meeting. The meetings do not have to be particularly formal, but they need to be on record. Someone will need to take official notes on what transpires. You can set up a corporation online or visit a capable attorney.

Fast Fact

Seven out of 10 consumers use professional car washes most often according to a 2012 survey from the International Carwash Association®.

Limited Liability Corporation (LLC)

Also popular with small-business owners, LLCs combine tax advantages of a sole proprietorship or partnership while offering the limited liability of a corporation. The overall management of an LLC is more informal than that of a corporation, there's less paperwork, and annual meetings are not necessary. Sounds ideal, right? Yes, but with these perks comes payment. LLCs are subject to self-employment tax which varies according to the business.

Claim Your Name

This is the fun part. Choosing a new name for your business should be enjoyable, but a little restraint is also required. You want your name to be unique, catchy, appropriate, and reflective of your mission. If you're shop is named *All Washed Up*, you are putting out a certain vibe to the community—funny, self-deprecating, not super professional. If you're business is *Drake's Custom Detailing*, you are going to come across as a bit more serious and committed to excellence. As they say, it's all in the name. Stay away from names with negative connotations in the automotive world like *T-Boned, accident, collision, dent, or rust.* Use your name to give customers a sense of who you are and what you provide.

So, who will you be?

Once you have selected the perfect name, it will be your business identity. A trade name is your official title and will appear on transactions, bank accounts, communications, and online material. All businesses must officially register their trade names unless they are sole proprietors and use their full legal name in the title. If you are *John J. Lambert Auto Detailing*, you don't need to register your title; however, a simple *Lambert Auto De-*

tailing will need to be legally documented—just a funny little loophole to remember.

Registration gives you exclusive use of the name but only in the area where you filed it. If you plan to extend your business outside your area through mobile detailing or franchising, you will need to file multiple forms, but when the registration expires, it can be easily renewed. A brief online search will give you an idea of what names are taken in the industry and perhaps some inspiration for an original one of your own.

Now let's talk branding. This is different from your name—it is your symbolic identifier. Take, for example, the television channel NBC. Yes, it stands for National Broadcasting Co., but I bet the first thing you envision when you hear the name is a little peacock with different colored feathers. That unique logo is part of NBC's overall branding and is what makes them recognizable.

In the beginning, you will probably be consumed in the process of finding customers and getting your business off the ground, but it's still important to think about your brand as it will continue to grow with your business. It's something you will want to create before you get larger and more popular. So, draft a logo and use it on everything related to your business, from print to online presence. Through word of mouth, marketing, and promotional activities, your brand recognition will grow and draw in more and more customer attention.

Loose Ends

In addition to naming, branding, and keeping it all legal, you will need to attend to a few other details before you can cut the ribbon off the front door or start the engine of your mobile business. Although small, they are mandatory:

- **Apply for an Employer Identification Number (EIN):** With the exception of sole proprietors who use their Social Security numbers, all business owners are required to have this federal ID number, which is used during tax time.

- **Comply with OSHA regulations:** Otherwise known as The Occupational Safety and Health Administration, this operation oversees everything related to workplace safety, including worker injury and illness. If a complaint is ever lodged against you as a business owner, you must answer to these guys. Penalties for workplace violations can be steep, so be sure to contact OSHA when starting up and find out how you can best meet their standards. If you are a sole proprietor and have no employees, you are exempt from OSHA rules, but it's always smart to play it safe nonetheless.

- **Understand Employment Law**: Any business that employs people must comply with Title VI of the Civil Rights Act of 1964, which prevents discrimination on the basis of race, color, or national origin. Employers must have all employees fill out a Form I-9 which verifies their eligibility to work in the U.S. As the boss, you also need to understand the Fair Labor Standards Act which governs the wages and hours of employees, dictates mandatory compensation, and ensures a safe, equitable work environment for everyone.

- **Observe Rules of Water and Waste Disposal**: As you know, car detailing uses a lot of water, and communities have different laws associated with how wastewater must be reclaimed or treated. Sometimes it can just run right into the sewer system, sometimes not. You will need to know the water details of your area in order to comply with regulations. Similarly, chemicals and other waste need to be disposed of properly, both for safety and for the environment.

- **Obtain a Business License**: Most places require a business owner to have a license. At the local level, this is mostly a formality fulfilled by a small fee. Your state surely has specific licensing requirements, so it's best to go online and find out what applies to you. If you have any questions, contact your state's division of licensing to find out more details.

- **Apply for Permits:** If you are planning to build, remodel, or just sell product, you will need a permit. In fact, you will need several. This involves paperwork and procedure, so be sure to find out what's expected of you by consulting an attorney or utilizing online government resources.

Hiring Business Advisers

Although new business owners need to watch initial expenditures, there are some things worth paying for — namely, the help of certain business professionals who are guaranteed to make your job easier and more successful. Let's be honest, you may be the most competent car detailer in the world, but it's pretty impossible to also be a computer savvy bookkeeper with a law degree that also has a knack for planning commercial spaces. Whew!

It's tricky to say, let alone do. It makes more sense to do the work you enjoy (and excel at) while letting others lend a hand in the more challenging areas.

- **Attorney**: Yes, all the jargon and legal speak can be intimidating, but that's precisely why you want a lawyer on your side. If you plan to be a small business owner, it's important for you to establish a working relationship with an attorney now, before you actually need one. Find someone you can trust and afford who knows the ins and out of your business. This person will become your confidant and advocate if things ever get legally troublesome. Not only that, your attorney can review contracts, help you sign a lease, look over zoning or building permits, and offer you sage advice on financial practices. To find a reliable lawyer, ask business acquaintances or friends if they have any recommendations or conduct an online search in your area for those with positive reviews.

- **Accountant**: Numbers, numbers, numbers. Are you good with them? There's a lot at stake when starting a new business and you don't want any mistakes when it comes to the money. Tax issues, bookkeeping, payroll, tracking income and expenses — these are critical elements of your business that cannot be left to chance. You want things to run as smoothly as possible, so find someone affordable and reliable. That said, make sure you always stay involved in the financial dealings of your business. Just because you find a dependable accountant does not mean you should ignore this aspect of your business. Stay involved!

- **Insurance Broker:** Granted, this person is not as vital as an accountant or an attorney, but you will want someone to call if you have a sticky insurance question or need advice about how to best structure your policies or find the most competitive rate. Considering you will need insurance for both your property and your employees, it's a valuable service. It can be both difficult and time consuming to slog through these issues on your own, so find a savvy consultant.

- **Computer Consultant:** Depending on your level of comfort in this area, you may not feel the need for someone in this department. Just remember, a business has a lot of computer needs from software installation to running specific programs to hardware setup to dealing with viruses. You may not have the time or energy to devote to this process, so it's wise to find a consultant who can come in when you need them and take care of it all.

- **Space Planner:** Unless you manage to locate a turn-key business where all you need to do is turn on the lights, you will want to plan out the interior of your shop. That's not to say you have hire a Feng Shui expert, but you do need to iron out the best way to configure a detailing area that's both safe and efficient.

Fast Fact

Experts have found that the average car needs about half an ounce of gasoline to get going. As a comparison, a shot glass holds an ounce of liquid.[6]

Insurance

One last thing to remember in this section is how to protect your assets. In building up your business, you also create a lot of value, and it's important to watch out for the fruits of your labor. Insurance is absolutely, positively key. A shop owner buys insurance to protect against risk and loss, and it is something you can't move forward without. An unexpected problem or

6. Mr. Magic Car Wash, 2014.

accident that is not covered by insurance can break even the most stable business.

As a business owner, the primary type of coverage you will need is commercial garage keeper's liability insurance, which covers client vehicles when under your care and also protects them against damage caused by fire, theft, or collision. You will also need property insurance for your building, worker's compensation in case an employee suffers a work-related injury, health insurance for employees, life insurance for yourself to protect your family in the event of your death, and possibly other smaller policies that protect you from theft. The trick about insurance is that you usually only need it when you don't have it, so plan ahead and cover all your bases.

Chapter 5: Finding Your Own Road Map

Given that we have been focusing on some of the smaller, more detail-oriented aspects of the job, let's step back for a minute and look at your business from afar. Before you start sudsing up any vehicles, you will need to cultivate a very important document: a business plan. This plan is like a road map — it will tell you where you are and where you are headed.

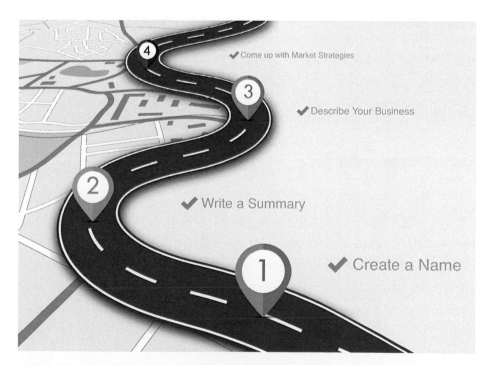

4 ✔ Come up with Market Strategies

3 ✔ Describe Your Business

2 ✔ Write a Summary

1 ✔ Create a Name

Sometimes, small business owners are so eager to just get started that they skip this step and never put their ideas into a master plan. Yes, it's good to make money and stay busy, but this developmental document is what gives you direction and keeps you on track for the future. Just as you wouldn't embark on a major road trip without some sort of map, you don't want to set out as an entrepreneur with no sense of direction. In both scenarios, you'll most likely get lost. So, how should you approach this?

Tackling The Business Plan

Before you begin overthinking this, don't. A business plan does not have to be particularly lengthy or detailed—it just has to be clear and concise. All you need to do is think about your business and how you envision it in the future. Regardless of whether you plan to stay small or grow over time, the basic components of a solid business plan are the same:

Cover sheet

Easy peasy—just write out the name of your company, the legal form of operation (sole proprietor or whatever), and the primary contact information for the owner, who will likely be you.

Executive summary

This is just a summary of the entire plan, usually less than a page in length. You should mention your business model (possibly including your nifty mission statement), the services you will offer, your legal form of operation, and your overall goals. The purpose of this document is to provide a glimpse of what your plan contains without having to read the whole document; it's just a summary.

Business description

Remember, this document will likely be viewed by others who are looking to understand your overall plan. In this section you will want to say more than just "I detail cars." You should discuss each service you provide, from your full detail service to your ala carte basics. You will also want to outline your business objectives here by focusing on goals that are specific, measurable, attainable, realistic, and trackable. Sure, you want to make a living and support your family, but these written goals should be ones that propel your business forward.

Market strategies

Remember in Chapter 3 when we discussed marketing and finding your target audience? Now is the time to use the information you gained through that process by making people aware of your services. Using everything from website material to word-of-mouth, you need to devise a marketing approach. You've got to get the word out that you are in the area and ready to offer some killer auto detailing services. This is an important part of your business plan because finding customers is half the battle.

Analyze the competition

By now you've already spent some time researching this aspect of your business, so it just needs to be included in your plan. You have hopefully already identified both your direct and indirect competition in the area, so now it's time to illustrate how you will rise above the rest. Refer back to the list of possible competitors in Chapter 1 and then think about the specifics of your business. You should list your competitors by name and think about how you are unique in relation to what they already do. It's your time to shine, so find a way to boost your image through a thoughtful look at why you are extraordinary.

Operational and management plan

What happens at your shop every day? This is just a description of the day-to-day operations of your business so you can explore the principles of what you are doing and give others an idea of how things run.

Financial data

This should include documents such as income statements, a balance sheet, and a 12-month cash flow breakdown. This also includes illustrating how your services perform and pay in order to generate profit. Simply put, this data creates transparency into the money side of your business for those who may need to understand it on a larger, more conceptual level.

Additional info

Is there anything else people might want to know about your business. Franchise information? Lease documents? Resumes? Partnership agreements? This is a good opportunity to sift through any pertinent documents, adding those that provide a more thorough background of your endeavor.

Don't forget: this is your business we are talking about, so take some pride in the process. Just like you work hard to make a car shine, take pains to make your business plan sparkle with error-free text and a professional presentation. If need be, have an experienced editor or writer look it over to ensure it's clear, correct, and impressive.

Once it's complete, put the business plan in a sturdy folder and keep it in a special place. As an entrepreneur looking for constant inspiration, you may want to consult it on a regular basis to check your progress and reassure yourself that you are, indeed, on the right track and headed for success.

Fast Fact

The average car has around 30,000 parts.[7]

Call For Help

Listen, if you are ever feeling stressed about any part of opening a new detailing business, the solution is easy—ask for help! If the mere thought of writing a business plan makes you queasy, don't fret. There are some excellent resources available to you at no cost, the first being SCORE Association, a national, nonprofit organization of executives who will provide free advice to aspiring business owners. You can find them online at **www. score.org**, just plug in your zip code and you're off to the races. If speaking to a real human is more your thing, they also have contact information on their site. You can also jump onto the website of the Small Business Administration at **www.sba.gov** to find useful hints on how to structure an effective business plan.

7. Mr. Magic Car Wash, 2014.

Chapter 6: Make Sure Your Lights Are On

Alright, with all this paperwork out of the way, let's get down to something a little more exciting—gear. As a car detailer, you know there can be a lot of equipment involved with making a car shine. Not only that, but you will need certain tools to keep your office and overall facility running smoothly. I don't have to tell you, however, that equipment and tools are not cheap, so be sure you take stock of what you already own before purchasing anything new. The word of the day is *budget*, so for now, just buy what you need rather than what you really, really want.

As a fledgling shop, you'll want to keep your startup costs as low as possible and may need to hold off on the big-ticket items until business is up and running. Once the dough start rolling in, you can treat yourself to that power tool you've been ogling for months. On the flip side, if the equipment you own seems out of date or in poor condition, you should consider replacing it in the name of efficiency and safety. Having reliable tools is essential. Just use your best judgment and think with your wallet instead of your heart. On that note, what *do* you really need to get started right away?

Exterior

- *Pressure washer*—Speaks for itself. Gotta have it.

- *High-speed buffer*—Used to remove pesky imperfections such as scratches and swirls, you'll need at least one of these in your arsenal of gadgets.

- *Random orbital/dual action polisher*—Used for applying and removing wax and sealants and filling in minor scratches, this bad boy is a value add.

Interior

- *Air compressor*—Used for cleaning small spaces and ideal for cars.

- *Carpet extractor*—Specifically for cleaning carpets, floor mats, and upholstery, this tool comes with a rotary brush shampooer perfect for tackling tough stains.

- *Wet/Dry Vacuum*—Slightly less powerful than a carpet extractor, this tool is a decent stand in until you can invest in an extractor.

- *Ozone odor remover*—This is a powerful piece of equipment used for removing odors related unwanted smells and destroying bacteria, viruses, and mold.

- *Odor fogger system*—This electric thermal fogger discharges chemicals into a car's interior to remove odors from pets, smoke, and food.

- *Interior dryer*—Used for speeding up post-detailing drying, this is a handy tool for the rush job.

Other Basic Tools and Supplies

- Stainless steel tank sprayer

- Foam pad cleaning tools

- Chamois drying cloth

- Wash mitts

- Nylon bug sponge

- Terrycloth or microfiber towels

- Spray and squeeze bottles

- Wire brush

- Nylon brushes

- Detail brushes

- Razor-blade scraper

- Single-edge razor blades

- Ultra-fine steel wool

- Sandpaper

- Heat gun

- Assorted polishing pads

- Finishing pads

- Wool and foam cutting pads

- Wax applicator

- Floor mats and seat covers

- Mechanic's creeper (for sliding under vehicles)

Detailing Products

- Car shampoo

- Tar and grease remover

- Adhesive remover

- Extractor shampoo (non-foaming)

- Stain removers

- Carpet and vinyl dyes

- Carpet shampoo (foaming)

- All-purpose cleaner

- Fabric protectant

- Leather cleaner and conditioner

- Clay bars

- Water spot remover

- Rubbing compounds (heavy, medium, light, microfine)

- Degreaser

- Tire and wheel cleaners

- Acid-free wheel cleaner

- Glass polish

- Dressing for tire, engines, and interiors

- Car polish

- Carnauba wax

- Paint sealant

- Chrome polish

As you can see, there are a lot of different products out there which means there are a lot of different brands. Remember, as a detailing professional, you should only use high-grade products that are strong and come in economy-size containers at wholesale prices. The best way to order any of these tools or products is likely online; however, you may want to seek out personal service when it comes to buying the more expensive and specialized equipment. Here's a few companies to jumpstart your shopping spree:

- Autogeek.net

- Detailing.com

- ChemicalGuys.com

- Detail King

- DetailPlus.com

- Kleen-RiteCorp.com

- Top of the Line

Downsizing Your Detail

Problem. What if you are planning to detail cars on the go with a mobile service? Some of these tools are heavy and difficult to move around. For the most part, you will be able to use all the same equipment as a regular shop; however, there are some places where it won't work. The answer is to purchase a mobile detailing trailer that is already fully equipped with all the things you need—power washer, generator, a place to stock products and tools, and a handy hook that attaches to the back of your vehicle. Boom—instant detail shop.

Fast Fact

The Small Business Administration recommends that you ask yourself 20 important questions before starting your own business. Examples of these questions are: *Why am I starting a business?* and *Who is my competition?* See the full list of questions here: **www.sba.gov/starting-business/ how-start-business/20-questions -starting**.

You don't need to worry about fitting equipment in your vehicle or finding a way to keep your chemicals safe and organized. It's a one stop shop and then you are free to move on to the real work. Depending on how it's outfitted, these trailers can range anywhere from $2,000-$10,000, but remember, this can also include the equipment. If you can afford it, it's worth the money, and the outside of the trailer will have a place for your company name and graphics (and branding logo!), effectively turning it into a moving advertisement any time you drive around the neighborhood. Here are a few online outfits you can check out before committing to a purchase:

- Details in Motion

- Detail King

- Detail Supply Outlet

- National Detail Systems

- DetailPlus.com

If you simply don't have the cash for this kind of trailer, there are other options. If you have a truck that you're willing to use for the business, you can buy what is known as a skid-mount wash system that fits in the truck's bed. You might also want to look into buying a standard lockbox for the flatbed so you can securely carry your supplies from job to job. Skid mount systems are also pretty easy to find online:

- Details in Motion

- Rightlook

- Ultimate Washer

Just remember, a mobile detailing outfit needs to be aware of wastewater, so also consider buying a reclamation system that consists of a vacuum system specifically designed to suck up recovered wastewater. These can also be found on many of the sites provided above.

Suiting Up

If you are going to be the boss, you have to look the part. No matter if you work alone or with numerous employees, it's important to appear professional while on the job. This can be easily achieved through purchasing some personalized, wrinkle-free shirts and hats. It's another great opportunity to put your branding out there for people to see, and it makes you look like a pro at the same time.

Although you may love your T-shirts, they don't always fit the part, so if you want people to take you seriously, you need to take your image seriously. These items are inexpensive and well worth the money, and the internet is swimming with businesses ready to provide exactly what you need. And while you're at it, don't forget to complete your overall uniform with appropriate eye and ear protection. You will surely be working with power tools and chemicals, so take the necessary precautions. Considering the amount of airborne particles, you may also want to invest in some disposable facemasks. All you need is a one-stop shopping place like **www.logosportswear.com.**

Feeling The Part

As a business owner, you will want to feel confident, organized, and in charge. There's no better way to do this than to properly rig out your head-quarters, otherwise known as your office. Believe it or not, you will spend a fair amount of time in there, so you might as well make it functional and comfortable. From paying bills to balancing the books, your office is your home when you're not working on cars. If you have the space on site, great, but you can also set up an office in your home which adds a bit more privacy and quiet. Either way, make sure the space caters to your needs and provides the appropriate setting. You will probably need:

- **Desk and comfy office chair**: Don't even think about using a dining room chair—you're going to want to be comfortable. Work is hard enough as it is without a backache. There's a bazillion deals to be had on eBay, Craigslist, IKEA, and at yard sales, so you shouldn't have to break the bank on a desk. You may want a filing cabinet to keep paperwork organized and some pictures on the wall to keep you happy. It's your place, so do what works for you.

- **A computer system with updated software**: Yeah, this isn't negotiable. These days, if you want to be competitive, you've got to invest in the right technology. If you choose to have a home office, you will definitely need a line used only for business, so don't try to use your home line for both. That's a recipe for disaster and a whole lot of confusion. Voicemail is obviously crucial so people can leave messages when you're not available.

- **Office supplies**: You need the basics—pens, notebooks, file folders, stapler, sticky notes—whatever makes sense to you. Use what you already have around the house and then just fill in the blanks with a quick trip to a local store or make an internet order.

Processing Payments

Unless you plan to operate a cash-only business, which isn't totally out of the realm of possibility for a detailer, you will need a merchant account that allows you to run payments from credit cards. You will also need the equipment associated with running the cards and have them connected to the bank for approval. This can also be done through accounting software like QuickBooks POS which essentially turns your computer into a receipt printer. Merchant accounts do have a service fee, but it is often worth the convenience it offers your customers. Search "merchant accounts" on the internet and see what turns up. You will surely find a fair, competitive offer perfect for a small business merchant like yourself.

It may also be necessary to join the 21st century through accepting PayPal or an online checkout system as a payment option. It will cost you a bit more to use these options rather than a merchant account, and your cash will not deposit instantly, but you can avoid time spent on swiping and running cards while the customer waits. Setting up a vetted and approved account before beginning makes it easy for customers to transfer funds directly to you and makes the whole process fairly hands-off.

Fast Fact:

Square, Inc. is a company that lets you accept credit card payments wherever you go. Read more at **https://squareup.com/about**.

Chapter 7: A Successful Road Trip

Are you a people person? Chances are, if you plan to be a small business owner, you will become very familiar with two important words: customer service. The customer is your bread and butter and the one to please. Building positive relationships through trust and communication is key for a detailer because a satisfied customer will be a returning customer!

Fun Stats—Did You Know? According to the Bureau of Labor Statistics . . .

- Consumers are twice as likely to share their bad customer experiences than they are to talk about the positive ones.

- It is seven times more costly to attract a new customer than it is to retain an existing one.

- Eighty-nine percent of customers stop doing business entirely with a company after experiencing poor customer service.

- It takes 12 positive customer experiences to make up for one negative experience.

- Seventy percent of buying experiences are based on how the customer feels they are being treated.

- A 10 percent increase in customer retention levels results in a 30 percent increase in the value of the company.

The Meet & Greet

Many professionals will tell you the initial meeting with a customer is one of the most meaningful steps in the detailing process. Taking the time to listen to a customer's needs is not just about being kind, but it's about creating an understanding based on trust. When you provide a service for someone, which they will pay for, you are establishing a working relationship that can grow and change over time and can become a very lucrative relationship in the right setting.

Take the time to look at their vehicle and hear their concerns; it's very possible you may be able to upsell them on additional services they didn't even know were available. As the professional, they are looking to you for guidance. This demonstrates both your competency and your willingness to help — two things they will greatly value.

Generally speaking, folks who have taken the time to bring their cars to your shop for detailing are probably pretty excited to hear any advice you might have on how their cars can be even better, so use this opportunity wisely. For example, if you have a detailing customer whose bumper is scratched after too many failed parking jobs, they may want to have that little repair taken care of as well. If you've already established a working relationship with a nearby auto body shop, you can quote them the price of a fresh bumper — while adding a 10 percent markup for your trouble, of course — and the customer will probably be pretty grateful for the convenience.

Fast Fact:

Seatbelts were first installed by car manufacturers in the 1950s.[8]

8. Mr. Magic Car Wash, 2014.

The Nitty Gritty

So, once the customer has unburdened themselves of their vehicle and their concern, what's next? What's the first step? It's best to begin with the inside of the car and work your way out. That way any dirt or contaminants stirred up from the cleaning won't blemish the fresh exterior work. Always start with a supply of clean, white towels and a receptacle nearby for collecting trash and soiled rags. If you keep your work environment clean and tidy and maintain a running list of all the areas you need to cover, you're sure to come out ahead.

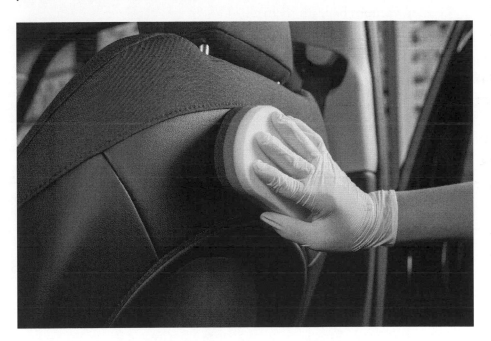

Interior detail: the procedure

- Remove and vacuum the floor mats thoroughly. Using a stiff nylon brush and a suitable stain remover, remove any lingering stains. Shampoo the mats and use a pressure washer or carpet extractor if needed to force out tough dirt or soapy residue. Set the mats aside in a visible location so you don't forget to replace them later.

- Bag up any loose items from inside the car, glove box, and center console. Always leave bag inside the car so it is not misplaced.

- Use a blower to remove dirt from hard to reach places, including under the seats and in crevices, vents, door pockets, and cup holders.

- Quickly vacuum the carpet to remove loose debris; perform another more thorough cleaning of the carpet and upholstery, paying close attention to pet hair.

- Flip up folding seats or take out removable back seats, blow out dirt, then vacuum beneath them all.

- Apply proper chemicals to remove spots on the carpet or fabric upholstery and scrub with a stiff brush.

- Collect the chemicals, cleaning tools, and towels you will need for the interior detail and sit in the driver's seat.

- Using a towel moistened with cleaner, gently wipe any dirt from the fabric attached to the roof of the car, otherwise known as the headliner. Do not saturate this cover, as it can loosen the glue that holds it in place. Clean as much of it as you can from your current position. You can clean the other half when you move to the passenger side.

- Clean the trim around the windshield and the door on the driver's side.

- First applying the cleaning solution to a pad or towel, clean the dashboard and around all the knobs and buttons on the instrument panel. Do not apply chemicals directly onto the dashboard, as it can drip into sensitive parts. Dry carefully.

- Scrub the steering wheel, steering column (including all knobs and levers), center console, and armrests.

- Shampoo the carpets after of the vehicle with a carpet extractor. Use paper or plastic mats to protect the clean, damp carpet after finished.

- Wipe the foot pedals with cleaner, but do not use rubber-dressing products because they may become slippery.

- If the upholstery is fabric, use the proper shampoo to clean the seats. Use the extractor once and repeat if necessary. If the interior is leather, do a patch test on an inconspicuous area before cleaning to ensure the product does not strip or discolor the leather. That would be a no-no!

- Run a clean, dry towel over the upholstery to remove as much moisture as possible.

- Shampoo the seat belts, removing spots if necessary, and clean the metal buckles.

- Wipe the door panel and spray all-purpose cleaner around the door jam and edge. Use cotton swabs or other small detailing tools on any stubborn stains or dirt. Wipe dry.

- Leave the car doors open to air out the interior and speed up drying time.

- Repeat the process on the front passenger side of the vehicle.

- Move to the passenger side back seat with all your supplies and begin the process of cleaning the rear interior.

- Clean the rest of the headliner all the way back to window.

- Clean the rear deck if applicable.

- Wipe the back seats first and then shampoo them, removing any spots.

- Wipe the side panels, the back of the front seats, and the headrests.

- Shampoo the back carpet and thoroughly clean the door panels, wiping down doorjambs.

- Move back to the front driver's side and apply dressing or leather conditioner to all leather or plastic if applicable.

- Spray proper cleaner on windows within reach and wipe dry. Give the windows a final polish with a dry cloth to remove any remaining streaks and spots.

- Move to the back once again and repeat this process.

- Deodorize the car interior.

Exterior detail: the procedure

- Use a pressure washer to wet the entire vehicle.

- Open the hood and wash the engine, starting at the top.

- Apply engine degreaser and scrub with a brush; rinse thoroughly with the pressure washer.

- Blow excess water out of the engine and compartment using an air compressor.

- Spray water-based dressing on the engine, then close the hood, letting it dry shiny.

- Use the pressure washer to wet the wheels, including wells and jambs.

- Apply wheel and tire cleaner on one side of the car. Scrub with the appropriate brushes and rinse.

- Move to the other side and repeat.

- Use a bug sponge to remove any critters from the front grill, fender, license plate, and backs of the side mirrors.

- By hand, wash the exterior with car shampoo, using a natural sea sponge or mitt. Never use cleaning tools with an abrasive quality. Start at the top and work in small sections to avoid recontamination. Rinse with pressure washer.

- Dry with a chamois or lint-free towel. Because water contains microscopic minerals that can scratch the vehicle's finish or eat away at the surface, do not allow water to dry on the paint.

- If present, remove spray from road tar or grime using a product formulated just for that job, and then wipe off thoroughly.

Trunk detail: the procedure

- Open the trunk and remove any loose items and bag the smaller items, setting them inside the car. Remove the spare tire if necessary.

- If possible, remove the carpet liner.

- Vacuum the entire trunk compartment.

- Apply spot remover and/or degreaser to the liner and scrub with a stiff brush. Wipe with a clean towel or use the extractor if necessary.

- Clean the lid of the trunk.

- Spray cleaner on the trunk jamb and wipe thoroughly.

- Shampoo the carpet liner either in or out of the vehicle.

- Wipe down all sidewalls of the trunk.

- Using the pressure washer, clean the spare tire by spraying it with dressing, rinsing, drying, and replacing it to its compartment.

- Spray dressing on a towel and clean any remaining rubber, including the weather stripping, as well as any plastic parts.

- Deodorize the trunk and replace the loose items.

The paint detail: the procedure

- If necessary, clay the vehicle by hand to remove paint overspray, surface rust, dust, and any other contaminants from the environment. Always rub in a circular motion.

- If needed, use a high-speed buffer and the appropriate compound and cutting pad to remove any scratches and oxidation. If not necessary, simply polish and apply a wax or sealant as will be described later.

- Working in small 2X2 foot sections, clean around the hood and around the vehicle. Keep the speed at 1,000 to 1,200 RPM, and be sure to clean your buffing pad frequently during the process.

- Use a buffer, polishing pad, and removal polish to get rid of swirls and compound scratches. Restore the vehicle's shine by using the same techniques just described. Fix small scratches by hand in tighter places by hand.

- Apply wax or sealant by hand, using an applicator pad or any kind of orbital waxer.

Finishing touches: the procedure

- Wipe all trim, tires, and bumpers again to remove excess dressing.

- Polish chrome, including emblems and tailpipes. Steel wool is especially useful for this purpose.

- Clean the edges and interior of the gas-cap compartment.

- Check for any remaining compound polish or wax in the cracks and crevices and remove it is necessary with a detail brush.

- Replace the floor mats in the trunk.

- Make a final inspection of the entire vehicle, then drive it into natural light or roll up the shop door to check for streaks on the windows or any material that was not fully removed. Apply a little "elbow grease" to correct any imperfections.

Granted, this is a lot to remember, but it soon becomes habit after you have detailed a lot of cars. Referring to this checklist in the beginning may be helpful, especially because customers will expect perfection when they pick up their shiny ride. It's always important to do the most thorough job possible. If you're a visual learner and would like to see some detailing tips first-hand, just look up some videos on the internet through sites like **www.youtube.com, www.autogeek.com**, or **www.meguiars.com.**

Chapter 8: Knowing When to Put Up the Top

Aside from knowing exactly how to do your job as a detailer, one of the most important steps you will face is locating the right space for your needs. Assuming you are not taking your show on the road as a mobile detailer, you will need a roof over your head and a shop to keep you working comfortably. Depending on your situation, this can mean a few different things; primarily will you lease or buy a building? Think about the scale of your business for a minute. Consider the number of employees you plan to hire and the amount of work you hope to accomplish in one day. Will you need a spacious shop that can hold three to four cars at a time or could a smaller shop still meet your needs?

Some detailers prefer to have a facility with a servicing area, hydraulic hoists, and even a waiting room, while others just need an open area such as a warehouse with good lighting and plenty of workspace. Obviously, this choice will depend somewhat on finances and what you can afford, but even frugal entrepreneurs can find just the right space once they understand their needs.

Finding The Right Space

Locating the right building for your detailing business is not so different from looking for a new home. You simply need to find a listing agent who handles commercial real estate and ask them to line up a few properties for your inspection. This may be already established shops or different garages that you can convert into workable spaces. These days, it's also a piece of cake to find potential spaces on the internet by just searching for businesses available in your area. Start looking for spaces nearby, and you will likely come across all sort of helpful information, especially the names of brokers who can assist you further.

Using a professional real estate agent is smart because they are a wealth of information and can guide you toward making the right choices regarding location, zoning laws, and the existing demographic. They will also likely have a sense of the competition and where your business is most likely to succeed in addition to what you can find in your price range. The very first choice you will need to make is whether you will lease or buy a space, as that will determine a great deal of your selection. After that, you just need to collaborate with an agent to check out the inventory in your area.

Leasing	Buying
Pros:	*Pros:*
Less money up front	You're the landlord
Not responsible for maintenance costs	Able to make any modifications
No overhead costs aside from rent	Tax advantages
Cons:	*Cons:*
Possible landlord issues	More money up front
May have limits on modifications	Responsible for maintenance costs
Need someone to handle repairs	Must cover overhead like insurance, etc.

So, what are some options out there that might work for a detailing shop? Sometimes it's helpful to get creative and think about different ways you can adapt a space to suit your purpose.

- Traditional standalone buildings are the most traditional and likely the easiest to visualize.

- Although a little harder to find, spaces inside other auto-related business such as a car dealerships or car washes are a great option.

- Large, open warehouses can be perfect if fitted with the right equipment for detailing.

- Self-storage units can also work as detailing hubs if there are no stipulations in your rental agreement.

- A defunct auto body shop or old tire shop could be perfect for your needs and will likely already have many of the amenities you need such as bays, hoists, and a working sewer system. Just be sure to identify why the business went under and if there are any issues that will affect your success.

- An abandoned gas station could also provide the right location; however, be sure they are not old enough to have any underground storage tanks that can threaten the groundwater and create unsafe situations in the future. It is possible to work with the government to remove and cleanup these old tanks, but that's probably not something you want to get involved in as you are trying to get your business off the ground.

Everything You Need to Know About...

The lease

When searching for the right building, you will likely encounter several different types of leases, some of which may simply be too expensive. Hopefully, there will also be some options within your price range, so let's take a look at some of the lease options you may encounter during your property search.

- A **gross lease** lets you to make a monthly rental payment while your landlord covers virtually everything else, including utilities, taxes, repairs, and maintenance.

- A **closed-end (or net) lease** allows you to pay rent plus a portion of the landlord's operating expenses, such as building maintenance, taxes, and utilities.

- A **triple-net lease** requires you to pay every cost related to the building in addition to the rental fee. In this situation, you lose many of the "pros" of leasing!

- A **shopping center lease** would be associated with a parcel of land or and outlet that is part of a larger shopping center or mall. In this case, your rent is tied to the square footage of the space, and you are generally required to pay for some maintenance of the common areas. And because your work area technically exists within a larger commercial space, you usually have to hand over a percentage of your gross earnings each month. Bummer, but if it is a location with pristine visibility that increases your overall business considerably, you may want to consider it.

No matter which type of lease you encounter, remember to always bring in an expert before you sign anything. There are just too many variables in a commercial lease for you to go it alone. Ask for help and always, always have your attorney review all documents before closing any deals.

Fast Fact

It takes 25 hours to build and manufacture a car, and 10 of those hours are spent painting it.[9]

The location

This is a consideration that cannot be taken lightly. It's permanent and will definitely affect the success of your detailing business. When making this decision, choose a building that will offer visibility, convenience and accessibility. After all, you want people to see your shop and notice your services. Make sure the street is well-lit, well maintained and offers customers easy access. It's not particularly important that the location caters to foot

9. **www.autoinsurance.org**, 2016.

traffic or offers parking; however, you may want to select a building near to other successful businesses, which can increase overall visibility and make your business part of a larger, thriving community.

The facility

Before you can even consider signing a lease, you will need to make sure the building you have selected is suitable for your needs. Don't settle for something just because it's easy; make sure it truly fits your vision. In general, most startup detailing shops need about 2,000 to 2,500 square feet to accommodate three vehicles before detailing, a waiting room with a counter and retail display, a storage room for products, tools, and large equipment; a small manager's office, and a customer bathroom.

By comparison, a bay that can hold about six vehicles would require about 4,000 square feet, and a 15-car business would probably demand about 7,000 square feet, possibly more. The bay has to be set up in a way that allows workers to move around comfortably, efficiently, and safely while working on cars from all angles. In most cases, about 75 percent of the facility should be designated as a work area.

The public area

When outfitting your shop, there's more to consider than just the fancy buffers and washers you will need. You need to think about the comfort of the customer who will also be using your facilities while you are working on their car. The waiting area should be given some special attention, making it both comfortable and welcoming. It should have comfortable chairs, a wall-mounted television with a decent number of channels, complimentary water, a table with some current reading material.

A small play area for children and free Wi-Fi are both great bonuses and will go over well with your customer base. They're a lot less likely to complain about wait time if they can work on a laptop or keep the kids occupied. Remember, the customer bathroom will need to be easily accessible from the waiting room and will require regular cleanings from either your staff or a professional service.

The retail space

Don't underestimate the power of products. If people are sitting in the waiting room for long periods of time, give them something to do—shop! You will need to purchase attractive wall-mounted shelves that can display your retail products, including cleaners, chamois cloths, deodorizers, or other car-themed gifts. These types of products are usually very affordable, and with the markup, can add a fair amount of profit to your business.

The signage

There's no better way to announce your arrival on the car detailing scene than with a large, well-lit exterior sign that is clearly visible from the street. Once you have your location, walk around the outside and check out where a sign would be most obvious. The sign can be relatively basic, although it must have the name of your business in large letters and hopefully a logo as well. Make sure the sign is lit even when you are closed, as it reminds the community about your services and locations at all hours of the day.

Yes, your electricity bill may be a bit higher as a result, but it's worth the additional advertising. Just make sure, before you spend any money, that you have permission from the landlord and zoning laws to erect your signage. As soon as you have the green light, put up that sign immediately— even if you are months away from actually opening your doors. It will get people talking and build excitement for the coming business.

Finding a mentor

Even though you may be feeling super confident about your impending role as a business owner, it's always smart to listen to the advice from those in the know. For example, take the advice of a successful franchisee who has developed his own territory by opening and selling five locations of detailing businesses. He employs many people and has a long list of regular customers who depend on his services. The guy knows his stuff.

Although he has lots of advice for new detailers, one thing he feels strongly about is the need for a good mentor. He didn't have one during his early years, and believes things would have been easier if he had just asked for help and advice from knowledgeable people around him. "I was a bit naive in those days and believed I could overcome anything," he said. "But this was my first business, so I had no idea what I didn't know. I probably would have done what I did anyway, but a mentor would have helped me go in with my eyes wide open." Makes sense. Now that he is older and more experienced in the industry, he is a mentor himself and frequently passes on advice to others who want to be successful in the same industry. So, be smart and take his advice too. Never be afraid to ask for help.

Fast Fact

Only 18 percent of the energy burned from the gasoline in your car reaches your wheels. The rest is lost due to heat, idling, friction, and accessories.[10]

10. **www.autoinsurance.org**, 2016.

Chapter 9: Choosing Your Pit Crew

Before we go on to discuss the value of employees and the many issues that surround being the big boss, it's worth it to state the obvious. Before you begin hiring people to help you in the business, see what you are able to accomplish on your own. Budget is the word of the day and will be an important factor when it comes to when (and if) you can hire others.

If your business progresses as planned, you will surely need help soon. Until that time, keep your costs low by working with as few people as possible. Once the customers start rolling in and the jobs become more plentiful, you can start thinking about hiring some employees to make things easier.

But how? Where can you find them? How much should you pay them? What are important qualities in an employee anyway? Before you even dive into these questions, remember a few things. Being a boss is challenging business — you have to exhibit strong leadership, deal with personality conflicts, manage schedules and time off requests, and provide adequate training.

Also, being responsible for another person's financial livelihood is nothing to be taken lightly — your employees are counting on you — and that can be a sobering experience for small business owner who already has other things to worry about. That said, when the time is right, you will be up for the challenge and ready to move forward with confidence. Here's how you can make that happen:

Find qualified people

They're out there; you just need to find them. For starters, you will likely need some detailing technicians who can perform labor and a act as a shop manager. Even though you are the big boss, having a manager who can oversee things like ordering products, scheduling appointments, and cashing out clients is a smart idea. They can also handle the general management of all the employees and work with them on scheduling and other day-to-day issues. Really, they are there to help you keep things running smoothly — so a manager is almost like a personal assistant. This assistance allows you, the owner, the freedom to pursue new business, market the operation, and even detail cars.

Technicians, on the other hand, are the workers that really make the business go, as they wash, wax, buff, and dress the cars. Although they don't necessarily need prior detailing experience, they do need the right dedication, commitment, and work ethic to learn fast and work efficiently. Just be sure whoever you hire is willing to listen and adhere to the protocol of your shop and take instruction without resistance. Remember, you can also choose to hire these people on a full or part-time basis depending on your needs.

Map out your employee search

As a manual labor detailing business, you are not required to pay people much more than the state minimum wage. While the financial convenience of this may be tempting, it can actually be harmful when searching for employees who will be trustworthy and responsible. Hiring employees is a lot like making an investment; you get what you pay for. Strength of character, reliability, and a sense of commitment are all traits you will want in someone who is managing your money and your livelihood, so consider compensating them fairly. They will work harder and likely stay longer, saving you the trouble of dealing with transient employees who leave for greener pastures.

Of course, you can search for employees in advertisements or online job boards, but it's likely you will get an avalanche of responses that will seem overwhelming. Instead, you may want to consider asking family or friends for referrals of suitable people who are looking for work. This will cut down the number of random applications you receive and provide you with a smaller, more fitting pool of people.

Be choosy

It's recommended to only accept applicants who have a high school diploma, a driver's license, a good driving record, and perhaps some work experience that in some way demonstrates their competency. Find a job application online that suits your needs (or create one of your own) and make sure all candidates fill one out so you can assess them for hiring. For their benefit, make sure you have drafted a job description for them to read so they understand the expectations of the role. This might sound a little silly for a job as straightforward as detailing, but clear communication and full disclosure are always highly recommended. You can also illustrate the challenges of the job and possibly deter any candidates who are not interested in working hard.

Interview people

Once you have identified some potential applicants, start the process with an interview. You should conduct an initial interview on the phone; however, you will want to personally meet any candidate you are considering for employment. During this prescreening phone interview, ask them a bit about their relative background and try to get a sense of their personality. Try to limit the number of possible candidates to a "short list" of four or five individuals—any more than that and they become blurred in your memory. Sticking to a smaller number also makes it easy to reach a decision.

Once you have your short list established, bring each one in for a face-to-face interview. If you haven't established a shop yet, meet someplace neutral like a restaurant. Always come to the interview prepared with questions and be ready to jot down some notes on each person to jog your memory later. At this point, you can ask the person some more direct questions about work history, interests, hobbies, and so on. Try to get a sense of who they are and if they would fit in with your professional scene. Just remember, you cannot ask a potential employee about their age, marital status, sexual orientation, political affiliation, or any other personal issue.

Stay away from questions that are discriminatory, and instead, focus on learning more about their professional abilities. Let them know what you will expect from them as an employee and share your job description again. They should be made aware of all aspect of the job, like hours, pay, and working conditions.

If your shop is up and running, give them a tour, and let them see the workplace. They can ask questions and find out more about the position. Before they leave, make sure to collect at least one personal reference and follow through with a phone call to find out more about them. You can confirm if their information is correct and hopefully a little bit more about their personality and work ethic. Don't hire anyone without doing this brief background check.

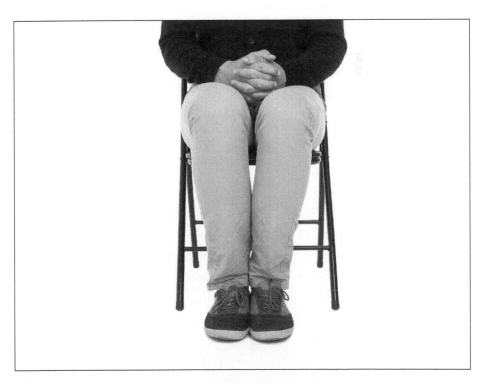

Cover your bases

Once you have hired someone, celebrate by having them fill out an IRS Form W-4 so the government knows how much federal income tax to withhold from their pay. Most states collect individual income tax, but there are few that don't. If your state does, go online and download the necessary form at **www.irs.gov/pub/irs-pdf/fw4.pdf.** As an employer, you are also required to have new hires fill out Form I-9, which verifies a person's identity and employment eligibility. All U.S. employers are re-quired to collect a completed form their employees, both citizens and noncitizens.

Once the form is done, the employee must present two pieces of identifi-cation as part of the verification process. Acceptable proof of citizenship or eligibility to work includes a valid U.S. passport or permanent resident card, copy of a birth certificate, or a Social Security card. Be sure to remind employees they must have this documentation on their first day of work! You will need to keep the I-9 on file at the shop for at least three years after the date of hire or one year after termination, whichever is later. It is a vital legal document that you must be ready to present at any time. A complete list of the documents suitable for proof of identity can be found on the last page of the I-9 itself.

Consider independence

As a small business owner, you should be aware of the independent con-tractors (ICs) who can offer a unique level of assistance. ICs are not actu-ally employees; they are just temporary workers who can be brought in to pick up the slack when you're extra busy. You can pay them an hourly wage, and you do not have to worrying about paying the employer's tax related to their work. Just don't think about trying to fool old Uncle Sam by calling all your works "ICs" in the hopes of escaping extra costs, as there are strict guidelines about how these workers are defined. Here's the criteria the government uses to determine a worker's status:

- *Behavioral*: How much control does the employer have over the worker?

- *Financial*: Are the business aspects of the employee's job controlled by the employer?

- *Type of Relationship*: Does a written contract of employment or benefits exist?

If any of these questions can be answered with a "yes," you have an employee, not an IC, and will need to treat them accordingly. Otherwise, there could be legal issues and stiff penalties such as heavy fines and even jail time. For more scare tactics, check out the Businesses section at **www.irs.gov** where you can download a copy of the IRS Publication 15-A, *Employers' Supplemental Tax Guide*. Moral of the story is: don't even think about tricking old Sam and don't mess around with the integrity of your business; it just isn't worth it.

Understanding Uncle Sam

Even though employees are crucial in helping you work more effectively, they are more expensive. This isn't just because of their salary, but because of the federal government. Employees create a tax burden on their employers—plain and simple. It's not their fault; it's just the way of business expenses. As the boss, you will be responsible for paying your employees (and possibly their benefit costs), as well as withholding certain taxes from their paycheck to give the government.

There is a specific formula for calculating exactly what employees should pay in federal, state, Social Security, and Medicare taxes, and it is really best left to an expert. Unless you feel very savvy in this department, you will want to hire an accountant who knows the law and how to handle this piece accordingly. It doesn't need to be your headache, but if you long to know more, consult IRS Publication 15, *Employer's Tax Guide*, and Publication 583, *Starting a Business and Keeping Records*, all of which can be downloaded from **www.irs.gov**.

But the tax fun really begins when you start ponying up your own taxes — namely the employer taxes. These include your share of the Social Security and Medicare tax, state unemployment tax (which varies by state), a self-employment tax on your own earnings, and the Federal Unemployment Tax. All of these can be read about in more detail online. So, yeah . . . Uncle Sam takes his cut, but that's just part of the process and an inescapable cost of doing business. Rather than stress about all the taxes, just find an experienced accountant who can help you navigate the territory and move on to what you do best — detailing.

Benefits to Benefits?

Being a cool employer and offering fringe benefits such as health insurance, paid vacations, sick days, and other perks might make you popular with your employees, but it won't let your business run smoothly. While it's important to take care of your workers, it's often not feasible as a new detailer to pay for a lot of amenities. According to the Discover Small Business Watch index, about 85 percent of small business owners who have less than five employees do not offer their employees' health benefits — it's simply too costly.

Although it feels unfortunate that an employer cannot always take care of their employees in this important way, the structure of health care system makes it very difficult. That said, if you do manage to reach larger, more secure status as an employer, providing health benefits for workers will do many things to strengthen your overall business and build a team of dedicated people who will likely stay with you for many, many years. Not only does your retention go up, but you will also have less training to do in the long run. You will also spend less money and time working with employees who are unsatisfied. If you can afford it, it's worth it to support the people who, in turn, support you.

One thing you can offer your employees to ensure their success is proper training. Working as a detailer requires a great deal of specific knowledge, and you will need to introduce new staff to the tricks of the trade and help them improve their own skills. For obvious safety reasons, they will need to understand how the equipment works, how products are used, and how they should handle themselves on the job. Without proper training, your employees will likely never meet your expectations.

Most training can be done right in the shop by either you or even the shop manager. If you feel weak in this area, you can also bring in companies such as Detail King who will offer training in their own facility to anyone looking to hone their detailing skills.

Safety First

Working as a detailer means you come into constant contact with various solvents and chemicals, which can affect your skin and your respiratory system if not handled properly. As an employer, it is your responsibility to make sure the work place is stocked with protective gear and clear guidelines for safety. In particular, this means making sure all employees have adequate eye and ear protection as well as a well-ventilated work space.

As mentioned earlier, a government agency known as OSHA will be very unhappy if you fail to meet these requirements. Lawsuits can be forthcoming — not to mention health problems. Since no one wants either one, take the necessary precautions and keep your workplace safe. If you ever want to know more about how to keep your shop safe, feel free to check out their site **at www.osha.gov** that offers a wide range of workplace suggestions. Some of the safety guidelines OSHA suggest for detailing shops include:

- Always report injuries immediately, no matter how minor they may be.

- Use the power of your legs, not your back, when lifting heavy objects, including machinery or large tools.

- Keep the work area clean and make sure any hazards are removed.

- Maintain tools and other equipment to keep them in good working condition. Remove any damaged or malfunctioning equipment immediately.

- Remove any jewelry and hazardous items before working with power equipment. Keep long hair tied back for safety.

Fast Fact

In Iowa, ice cream trucks are illegal.[11]

11. **www.autoinsurance.org**, 2016.

Chapter 10: Getting a Noticeable Paint Job

Once your building situation is locked own, you are ready to move on to really selling yourself. Even though the products are shelved and the equipment is ready to go, it's no good without some business. Bottom line is, you have to get customers through your front door, and the best way to make this happen if through advertising.

Back in Chapter 3, you learned a few things about identifying potential customers and targeting the market, but you will need to give a little more thought to the process before you can take off. Advertising can be expensive, so it's important to understand what practices are most effective for car detailers in particular and how you can begin launching your very own small business campaign.

Buying Visibility

Although no one loves the word *budget*, it will become a pretty important word in your entrepreneurial world. As a new business owner, you will likely have to give about two to five percent of your gross monthly sales to advertising. At a point when you don't yet have any sales, this can feel like a hefty amount. But before you scoff and consider not doing it, remember this is probably your best shot at generating a real profit. Rather than worrying about why it has to be done, let's focus on how.

Brochures

There are two different types of print advertisements available in today's world: those that are on paper and those that are on the internet. They both have value, but one of the best ways to start strong is to create a brochure for your business. Magazines, newspapers, and billboards are also great ways to reach customers. However, they need to be repeated often to make an impression and are usually quite costly. Brochures are affordable and easy. They can be handed around at events, left at other local businesses, and generally shared with people who may someday soon be customers.

Making a brochure is pretty basic. They can be configured in many different ways and come in lots of shapes and sizes to suit your needs. But what they all have in common is the ability to help you get off the ground as a new business. This is your chance to make a strong first impression, so the brochure should definitely include:

- A service menu describing all the detailing packages you offer

- Full contact information for the shop

- Photos of beautifully detailed vehicles

- A map with directions to your business

- Possibly some customer reviews

Places like FedEx Office, AlphaGraphics, and OfficeMax can all produce impressive brochures with glossy stock paper. If you live in an area that does not have a speedy print shop nearby, try an online print service instead, such as Vistaprint or Smartpress. They often have nifty templates where you can drop your pictures and copy right in, immediately providing a preview of what the product will look like. If you are willing to pay a bit more, you can even get custom design with your personal logo! No matter the selection, you will find internet orders tend to be a bit lower in price than real print shops.

Fast Fact

The website Fiverr (**www.fiverr.com**) provides logo design services starting at $5.

That all sound nice, but maybe you don't know what you want. Sometimes, when designing something, an initial decision can be the hardest part. If you've never created one before, start by collecting a number of brochures from various businesses (and competitors!) to get a sense of what you like. Look through a wide variety to really understand your options. Two-color? Textured stock? Slick and glossy paper? You should take the most appealing aspects from all your choices and put them together to create something that demonstrates who you are and what your business can do.

Let your brochure really speak for your services and entice people to enter your shop. Before you can print it, you will need to generate some copy for the inside. Think about what's important to tell your customer base and write it down.

Ask yourself:

- Is my company an industry leader?

- Does my business have a market niche?

- What distinguishes my company from my competitor?

- Do we offer better value, service, or selection of products?

- Do we have anything new or different to offer?

Remember:

- Your target audience.

- The message you want the customer to receive.

- The level of sophistication you want to put forward.

- What kind of brochure design you like.

- What type of photographs or illustrations can best convey your message?

- What format

Definitely don't forget to include:

- Mailing address

- Phone number

- Fax number

- Email address

- Website URL

- Hours of operation

Once you know what you want to say and depending on your writing ability, you may want to hire a professional writer to produce some sparkling copy. After all, once it's printed, it will be a permanent and highly useful resource for your business. Considering it's often the first thing people see, it needs to be clear, correct, and engaging. If you have any concerns about your brochure, have a qualified person evaluate your ideas and give feedback. You want to give it as much thought as possible before spending money on printing.

Postcards

 This type of advertising may be basic and simple, but it can be extremely effective. Possibly the biggest workhorse of the advertising world, the postcard is inexpensive, unpretentious and provides plenty of space to convey a strong business message. And there's room for a picture! Everyone knows people are more likely to flip a postcard over and read the message, even if it's an advertisement, just because their curiosity can be met so easily.

Detailers use postcards to announce grand openings, offer special deals, describe services, and provide an overview of the business. They come in a few different sizes, all of which are perfect for mailing. Even though we live in a technology-driven society, the U.S. mail service still offers a lot of value to a business owner.

Once you have a mailing list, you can easily send out your postcards to potential customers. You can find many different list brokers online who can help you fatten up your mailing list if you're interested. You can also generate lists by "renting" them from places like the DMV and utility companies. And of course, you should be gathering addresses of customers as well to bump up your numbers. Just remember, no one wants to be flooded with advertisements, so use the list with care.

Fliers

Another inexpensive, low-key way to advertise is through fliers. They can be printed on affordable paper in one color and easily designed using a variety of online word programs. Once printed, you can tuck them under windshield wipers, slip them under office doors, or leave them under door mats. Just make sure you don't hand them out in illegal areas where permits are required, and never, ever put them in someone's mailbox. Those are considered federal property and should never be tampered with, even for advertising purposes.

Discount coupons

Everyone loves a bargain, right? Detailing customers are no different, so try offering some kind of coupon for a free service, like a fluid top-off with every detail or a certain percentage off some of your pricier packages. Giving discounts is a great incentive to get customers in the shop and get them hooked on the joy of a perfect detailing experience. Once you lure them in and do an excellent job, they'll keep coming back. Not to mention, customers often upsell themselves once they are in the shop, buying products or adding on extra services they like. Great places to distribute your coupons are car shows, car washes, car dealers, or any other place where cars are on the brain.

Door tags

The little advertising gems are remarkably cheap and can make a big splash if done correctly. They must be printed up and then can be hung from any doorknob, an effective way to boost your initial visibility. You can also spread the love around by hanging them from the rearview mirror of a freshly detailed car.

Online

 The internet may be your best friend when it comes to visibility. Online billboards known as "banner ads" are very effective, as people can get their information at no cost. You will want to go online and check out possible opportunities for online advertising before you do anything else. See what you can afford there and then, if the budget allows, you can expand into other avenues.

Facebook is also a great place to start if you're on a budget. Set up a company profile and start running highly-targeted advertisements for as little as $5 per day. Learn how to create an ad here: **www.facebook.com/business/help**.

Website

Doesn't everyone have a website these days? Even though it might seem like cyberspace is filling up fast, there's plenty of room for your business online. Having a professional website for your business is absolutely mandatory. It will be one of the first places customers go to find the details of your details. Savvy customers jump online when they need just about anything, so if you're not out there to offer it up, you'll miss out on a great deal of business.

Fast Fact

Though creating a highly advanced website is a great idea for a long-term business, starting out with a free blog might be your best bet. Sites like Wordpress and Blogger can be a great place to showcase your work for no initial investments.

Step I: Again, just like paper print ads, you will need to create some killer content for your site. This is probably best done through a professional writer who can make it sparkle and shine. You want to produce a site you can be proud of, so don't skimp on this piece. If your copy is poor, it will reflect badly on your business as a whole. Website content should be relatively brief and to the point, probably just one screen page. You don't want to overwhelm people with too much information. The great thing about a website is how limitless it can be. You can include your copy, pictures, information, maps, reviews, and the like. Customers can email you through your site, and you can provide a link on your homepage that will connect them easily with this feature.

To up the convenience factor, set up your site to allow customers to book appointments online and provide a shopping cart where they can make online purchases. Just remember, if you do offer this feature, you will need to prep your shop for shipping out products, which can add a whole new layer to your work.

Step II: When it comes to designing the site, however, this is a task best left to the professionals. If you feel like you are knowledgeable and have the time, you could complete this piece yourself, but it seems likely you will have a lot of other responsibilities on your plate. Hiring a web designer who can manage the whole thing for about $2500 is one of your best options—and once it's done, it's done. If possible, try to find someone who can handle the whole endeavor, from website maintenance to content management.

Step III: Once the website is created, the next step is to optimize it in cyberspace by inserting keywords into the site language. Keywords are search words that lead people to your website when they use certain search engines. This process of improving the quality of hits on a website is known as search engine optimization (SEO) and helps put your business at the forefront of search-engine results. The key is to make sure your website comes up as quickly as possible during a search, and this is done through SEO optimization. When you hire a content writer for your site, be sure they are aware of this piece and can offer that service.

SEO Example:

For example, when a customer searches for "detailing," about 133 million hits will pop up, many of which will not be related to car detailing all. If the search is changed to "auto detailing," the search will be narrowed to about 24 million sites. When the search expands even further to "auto detailing Denver," the number lowers even more to say 1 million, a number which can't possibly be a true representative of how many details are in the city of Denver. Some of those hits are happening simply because the individual words are listed somewhere on a website. Next, the search can be specified even more with "auto detailing metro Denver," which will narrow the search to near 215,000. Now you are getting somewhere. Add any other relevant search words like a street name or a service, "auto detailing metro Denver claying," and you will begin to see even more specific results. So, as you can see, the more keywords you enter into your site, the more likely someone will find you.

Step IV: Time to select a domain name. This is another important part to the SEO process, as it is essentially your website's address (or URL). Usually detailers name their businesses after themselves, as in Dan Tanna Detailing, which translates to a URL of **www.dantannadetailing.com** on the internet. If the .com URL is not available (which is likely), you can try to get an extension like .net, .us, or .info. Just because there's a trend of naming a shop after yourself, does not mean you need to follow it. Pick a name that works for you. When you are ready to select your domain name, go to a provider like GoDaddy.com, where you can type in your chosen name and check its availability. Be prepared with a few different names because the internet is a busy place. Domain names are registered in one-year increments for about $10 per year.

Sponsorship

This can be particularly effective if you live in a small community where word of mouth is strong and people pay attention to local activities. For example, sponsoring a school athletic team can bring a lot of visibility to a small business and generally generate morale around your brand. By picking up the tab for the uniforms, you will likely have the name of your business emblazoned on the jerseys and across any related print material. That means any time your team heads out onto the field, you get a few hours of effective advertising and a lot of appreciative smiles.

Trinkets and trash

For years, marketers have fondly referred to specialty advertising items imprinted with a company's name, logo, and contact information as "trinkets and trash." Trinkets maybe, trash? No way! These items can make it into the pockets and purses of many people, including prospective customers who will be reminded of your shop name every time they see them. Think pens, water bottles, key chains, license-plate frames, sunshades, and travel mugs. Pick items that people use often or that are associated with driving. These items can be purchased in bulk and handed out like candy to those who may come a-calling.

Business cards

Although humble and somewhat old fashioned, business cards are actually quite powerful little tools. They can be distributed far and wide and left in many little spots for interested eyes, like counter tops in your shop. They can be handed out in social or business situations or included in mailings. Business cards are inexpensive yet very effective. They are straightforward and easy to design, so it's really kind of a no-brainer. Check out a popular business card website such as Vistaprint or Smartpress—they have tons of templates to choose from if you don't know how to design your own.

Remember, you can always get creative with advertising. There are always television spots or radio, both of which might be viable options once you start turning a decent profit.

Chapter 11: Getting People to Notice Your Sweet Ride

Guess what? There are a few more advertising secrets you need to know. There are some really useful tools out there for increasing awareness in your business for next to nothing. This inexpensive (and often free!) publicity can provide some needed help for an entrepreneur and can often be just as valuable as expensive advertising.

Some people will tell you it's not wise to spend any money on advertising until you have established your presence and brand in the market. To a cash-strapped entrepreneur, that might sound like a darn good idea; however, the reality is, you need to employ ads as well as whip up some carefully planned publicity for yourself.

When you create publicity materials, you are just hoping they get into print or on the air. That's right, *hoping*. Unlike advertising, which is more of a slam-dunk, there's no guarantee your efforts will be recognized. That said, publicity efforts could give your business a tremendous boost when they work properly. Let's explore what that means exactly.

Newsletters

These are very useful tools for keeping customers in touch with your services and products. Once you invest in a software program with newsletter templates, your cost to produce regular communication will be very low. An even less expensive option is to send your newsletter electronically (and even better for the environment). Either way, these are some topic you will want to cover:

- *Description of services*

- *Information about vehicle care packages you offer*

- *Stories about weather-related or seasonal care-care issues*

- *Reviews of the detailing products you sell and a brief description of how to use them*

- *Information about car clinics you conduct or endorse*

- *News about local automotive activities*

- *Details about participation in charitable events*

- *Testimonials from satisfied customers*

- *Details about your customer referral program*

- *Newsletter subscriber-only coupons and specials which will build up mailing list*

Newsletters don't have to be long; they just have to be clear and informative. One standard page with two sides is probably plenty. You only need enough space to make readers enthusiastic about your services and detailing packages without overwhelming them. In fact, you can just use one side of the newsletter if that's enough but leave space on the bottom third of the reverse side so you can attach a mailing label there instead of stuffing envelopes. If you are electronically sending your newsletter, which is brilliant alternative, you won't even need to work about this. You might want to consider doing both, as some of your older customers may not be as internet savvy as the younger set and would appreciate a printed copy.

You can write the newsletter yourself or have the shop manager create it—even better, have a freelance writer draft it for you. No matter what you decide, remember the language in your newsletter reflects on your business, so choose wisely. If your newsletter is sloppy, people might assume your work is, too.

Fast Fact

You can post any freelance jobs on Upwork (**www.upwork.com**). Here, freelancers will bid on your project, helping you to find the most qualified and inexpensive path to a well-written and professional looking newsletter.

Be sure to put out your newsletter regularly—monthly, every season, whatever. It will make less of an impact if it is erratic, as it appears to be an afterthought and not particularly important. Your shop is important and should be well-represented. Treat this material as an essential part of your marketing strategy and build an archive of newsletters on your website for customers to peruse for tips and information. This is an easy way to drive customers to your website and remind them what you can do.

Email Communication

Considering how important online presence is these days, this piece warrants a bit more discussion. Once you have a website up and running, you can consider sending communications through this platform; it's cheaper and less time consuming. Email is typically shorter and does not contain full-blown articles. Rather, it includes brief introductions to each story, about one paragraph long, attached to links for more information. Although those links should transport readers to your website, they should not take them to your home page. You don't want to confuse people or make them work too hard for the information. They will expect to click right to the article itself on the site.

News Releases

 Otherwise known as a press release, this is a promotional article about two pages in length. It focuses on positive news in the business and what has been going on at the shop that people will want to know. Let the world know what you've been up to and why they need to bring their car in pronto! Garner enthusiasm by mentioning:

- *Your exciting grand opening*

- *The charitable and community activities you are involved in, including contributions you make to local organizations or sponsorships you are supporting*

- *Workshops you are teaching on the art of detailing*

These blasts should be short and pithy, because the people who receive them will likely just give them a glance. As a result, it's important to have a catchy headline and attention-grabbing first line. You can send this material to a news outlet but there's no guarantee it will appear in print. If the local sources find room in their format, it may work out, but it's a gamble.

If you're looking for a news release template, check out online sites through a simple search. There are many, and they will guide you through the simple formatting of a news communication. It goes without saying, any time you develop written content for your business, be sure to use a persona who knows how to write. If you did want to do this yourself, just remember these bits of essential information:

1. Who?

2. What?

3. When?

4. Where?

5. Why?

6. How?

Networking

If you have ever attended a job fair, you already understand the power of networking. It brings people together who are in the same business and are looking to contact on a larger platform. By getting to know other detailers and their situations, you can identify your own brand better and connect with the industry as a whole.

Venues such as roundtables, meet-and-greet events, socials, parties, and the like are perfect places to hand out that nifty business card and meet like-minded individuals. You will be surprised at the way you can improve your condition as a business owner through discussing bartering, trades, or current trends in the market. You will learn a lot.

Public Speaking

Some people are positively terrified at the prospect of public speaking and would rather be swept away by a tornado than talk in front of others. But as a business owner, you need to find a level of comfort in speaking on a more public platform. You are an expert in your industry and someone who has the ability to offer valuable information, so people will want to hear from you. By demonstrating your confidence and vast knowledge, you will also convince the public that you are the one for the job.

Fast Fact

Public speaking is ranked No. 5 on a list of things Americans fear most. Walking alone at night and identity theft top the list.[12]

There are a lot of opportunities to wax poetic about your profession. Let's start with offering a car-care clinic at your shop or offering a few words before a sponsored little league game. You will also find that business organizations, libraries, car clubs, and even churches are sometimes looking for speakers to fill a hole in their program. It just takes a few phone calls and some decent networking to line something up. You may also be able to teach a one-time class on detailing at the local community college.

12. Chapman University, 2014.

You never know—you might meet a few students who would make excellent new employees. Why share your detailing secrets with a non-paying audience? Simple: they may have interest or desire but no time to actually do it. They may decide, after hearing the level of work, to pay someone else. Either way, this means business for your shop. And don't forget your business cards!

Fundraisers

Yet another way to get the world out, the fundraiser is a great way to position yourself as a caring community leader (which you are!). Whenever someone approached you with a request for a detailing service to be auctioned off or offered as a raffle prize, especially if it benefits a nonprofit or other worthy organization, say yes.

You will win on many levels: the organization will be eternally grateful, you will gain helpful exposure, and your business will become a respected aspect of the community. Best of all, you don't have to pay out of pocket for this visibility, and it's an excellent way to drum up business. You simply do what you do best—detail cars—in exchange for the promotional opportunity.

Viral Promotion

 No discussion of free promotion would be complete without touching on the power of social networking sites. They are becoming the tools of choice for promoting a business network with other professions and creating additional visibility to the community.

Facebook

Probably the most popular of all the platforms, this site allows you to create a profile for your business that is separate from your personal life. Customers or followers can then access that page and "Like" it, which means they will then receive whatever updates you post on their feed. On your business page, you can post pictures, video, and associated information, so you essentially have a public spot where people can view your business outside of your personal website.

Your Facebook page can provide a link to that as well, and it allows you to post updates about your shop at any time, all of which will reach anyone who is following you and is looking at their news. This may include an announcement of specials, holiday hours, or anything buzzworthy you want to share. It's just one more promotional tool that can draw people back to your website and then to your shop where they may end up paying for services. It's very possible to reap the benefits of Facebook without spending a penny, so why wouldn't you?

Twitter

This micro-blogging system can help you keep in touch with customers and form a professional development network. Twitter posts messages of up to 140 characters or less called "tweets" for your followers (people who have chosen to join your network). You can also post photos, audio clips, gifs, and even live video. So, let's say business is slow and you are looking to land a few more jobs before the end of the day. You could send a tweet out to your network telling them "Take 15 percent off interior detailing for the next three hours!" It's entirely possible you will grab at least one more gig.

Instagram

Just like FB, you can create an account for your business and send out occasional blasts to your followers, updating them with a nifty pictures or even video regarding what's in your business. Pump up the enthusiasm!

Blogs

Before social media, there were blogs. These are personal, online entry-style sites usually attached to a company website with no particular length. Blogs contain commentary, opinions, insights, information, facts, news articles, and other pertinent content. It is usually a blogger's intention to create a following for their business or endeavor, which means the content has to be scintillating on some level and relevant to what readers want—otherwise the blog will be left unread.

Business owners use blogs in different ways. Sometimes, they are used to drive traffic to their website and sometimes to stimulate sales. A detailing blog on your website would be a great way to promote and build excitement for your services and products. You can use your blog as an online newsletter or as a forum to comment on issues of interest to the detailing community and consumers.

However, it's not enough to occasionally dump some information on your blog and leave it at that. It needs to demonstrate attention and care. If you truly want to use it as a marketing tool, it will need to be done by a professional writer who can capture the voice and tone you are looking for with sharpness and attention to detail. It is worth noting, there are now more than 100 million blogs on the internet which may dampen your enthusiasm. Just remember, unless you are a writer yourself or know one, you will need to pay someone to keep it up and running.

Fast Fact

Hummers are the cars with the highest ticket rates.[13]

Grand Opening Celebration

Out of all the promotional techniques discussed here, this will cost the most but may also make the biggest splash in terms of impact and visibility. The good news is you can pull off an interesting and exciting grand opening to introduce yourself and your services to the community without spending a fortune. Just lay out some refreshments like coffee, sodas, cookies, or even hot dogs and have some promotional items on hand.

Put the word out (jump on Facebook!) and invite friends and family to come and support you on the big day. Choose a good date that doesn't interfere with holidays or school break and be sure to spread the word as far as you can. Make sure the staff can be present and the shop is in tip-top shape for the big day. Unfortunately, this option really only works if you

13. **www.autoinsurance.org**, 2016.

have a building to use for the celebration. If not, try some other promotional strategies instead.

The centerpiece of your grand opening should be a hands-on demonstration of your detailing abilities. If possible, arrange the shop so you have a staging area. Place rented chairs in front of it in rows so people can watch the demo. If that doesn't work for your space, park the vehicle to be detailed in the center of the area and allow people to crowd around it. If it's a nice day, this should definitely happen outside in the sunshine.

Make sure you have a few key employees around to answer questions and provide explanations. To keep the kids busy, offer face painting, balloons, or even a bouncy house—anything that can offer up a family-friendly day. You should have plenty of promotional material on hand for interested guests and plenty of cool products on display. Put a stack of business cards and brochures, maybe run a raffle for a free detail, and start partying!

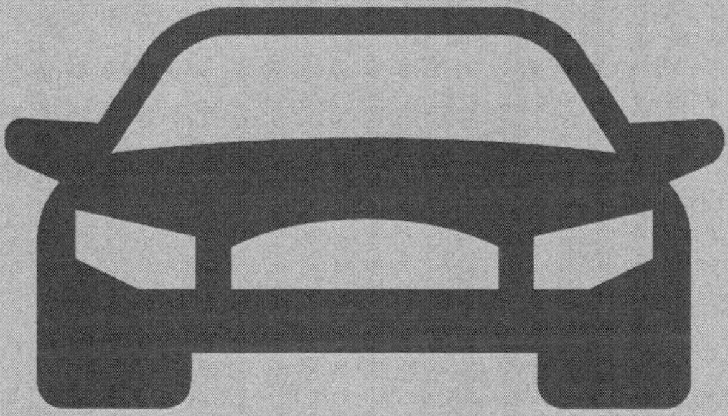

Chapter 12: Paying Your Gas Bill

One of the reasons a car detailing business is so attractive to entrepreneurs is because you can start on a shoestring budget. Yes, this is true, but even the most frugal one-person show will need more than just a bucket of soapy water and a sponge to run a detailing shop well. In reality, you will need some financing to keep the business going during any initial sluggishness.

As you know, it's easy to sink a lot of cash into detailing equipment, tools, and supplies, but you can start making money with just the basics. Low startup costs really do equate to greater business success because you are not starting out with a gigantic financial liability that can drag you down.

You want to run it lean and mean until you are really on your feet and are turning a regular profit. The same thing goes for recurring overhead costs — keep them down. You want to increase your chance of success, even in a slow market or during months of inclement weather. So, what are the back-office expenditures, operational expenses, and human resource costs you are likely to encounter during the startup phase?

Mortgage & Rent

This is a big one, and it can't be avoided unless you divinely inherited a building or decide to work out of your garage for a while. It's a tricky decision — while it's financially wise to put this off as long as possible, it's also essential to get some kind of shop set up. The truth is, do it as soon as you can but don't stretch your cash so far that you run out.

How much you will pay each month for this piece depends entirely on where you live and how extravagant you want to go. Figure out how much space you need and start looking into properties to rent or buy, depending again on your budget. Consider variables like square footage, car capacity, and number of potential employees. Once you can settle on a basic monthly cost, you can figure out the timing on what you can afford.

Utilities

You must include this cost in your monthly overhead because electricity, gas, and water are just kind of really important. You can't run your detailing business without them. If you are leasing a space, your landlord may include some or all of these costs in your monthly rent payment; otherwise, you are responsible for them. If you are working out of a facility that you own, you need to calculate the cost of the utilities used to maintain your household vs. the cost incurred by the business. The easiest way to do this is to refer back to the pre-business utility bill of the property and estimate what percentage of the bill can be attributed to business use.

Fast Fact

The first speeding ticket was given in 1904 to an Ohio driver for going 12 miles per hour.[14]

Employees

For some small-business owners, adding workers to the payroll is a real sign of success. If you have so much business that you need help, that's a good sign, right? Maybe. The reality is that an overstaffed business sucks cash and can quickly go under. Employees are expensive, both because of salary and taxes, not to mention they require your time for management and training. But they are obviously wildly helpful when it comes to getting things done faster and more effectively. Just remember to give the matter a lot of thought before hiring someone, and make sure you are going to get enough assistance out of the relationship to warrant the new expense. You'll want to consider things like hourly pay and taxes.

The current minimum wage lingers around $7.25 an hour, though many states are expected to raise their minimum to $12-15 per hour within the next few years. Therefore, a part-time worker who puts in 20 hours a week

14. **www.autoinsurance.org**, 2016.

will earn about $145, while a full-time worker will make about $290. That works out to $580 a month for the part-timer and $1,160 a month for the full-time employee.

This is the absolute lowest you can expect to pay anyone, and it is worth mentioning that many detailing shops pay considerably more. Be sure to check out what the competition pays their employees before deciding on the lowest rate. You will want to be as fair and equitable as possible, especially considering how valuable employees become over time.

Taxes

For every wage earner on the payroll, there is an unavoidable tax liability that may hinder your ability to meet your obligations. These include but are not limited to Social Security, Federal Unemployment, Medicare, and Workers Compensation. To find out more about the specifics of taxation for small business owners, check online at **www.irs.gov**. Just as guideline, here's an example of what one full-time employee might cost a month:

Wage:	$1,160
Combined Taxes:	$174.31
Total:	$1,334.31

Owner Salary

Yahoo! Finally, some good news. You get to make money, too. Now, some entrepreneurs choose not to take a salary in the formative years of their business, opting instead to plow all the profits right back into the business to ensure success. Sounds nice, but there are those pesky expenses of personal bills, family, and food to consider. Perhaps a somewhat limited salary would be a decent idea, at least for the first few months.

Benefits

Offering fringe benefits such as health insurance, vacation time, sick pay, and retirement plans are a wonderful way to attract and retain dependable employees, but the reality is, you may not be able to afford such luxuries, at least for now.

Monthly Service Charges

Mortgage and rent payments along with personnel costs will eat up a big share of your monthly expense budget, so the operational charges you will see may look pretty small by comparison. Among these costs, you can expect:

- Telecommunications: This includes the cost of landlines for voice and fax communication, as well as cell service. Even if you are starting a mobile-detailing shop or a garage-based operation, don't make your cell phone double as a personal and business line. You need to have a dedicated business phone, so as to appear professional if nothing else. A landline with voicemail is fine. If you don't want a traditional landline, at least spring for a second mobile phone, which you can use when you're on the job.

- Online Charges: These include the cost of online services like Wi-Fi and web-hosting costs. If you plan to engage the services of a web-master or content writer, you can include their hourly fee here.

- Accounting Services: It's safe to say you will need the services of a qualified accountant or bookkeeper for a couple hours a month, both to keep track of your accounts receivable and payable and to make sure the business taxes and tax filings are submitted on time.

- Legal Services: Most start up business owners will not need to have an attorney on retainer, but you never know when an employee might damage the finish on a prized Mustang or when a customer might slip on an oil slick and fall in your shop. In defense, allocate funds every month, even if they are only on paper and will lounge comfortably in your bank account. A modest figure such as $50-$100 a month should suffice.

- Merchant Account: This is an inescapable necessity for even the smallest detailing company because of today's credit/debit-dependent society. While it's not unheard of for a client to whip out a few crisp Benjies to pay for a full detailing job, they are more likely to break out the plastic instead. Among the many fees associated with merchant accounts are: *transaction fees, processing fees, internet gateway fees, retail discount fees, chargeback fees, statement fees,* etc., and there are probably more that haven't been invented yet. In general, the statement probably comes in around $50 a month just to host the ability to run these cards.

- Check Verification Service: Society has been moving toward plastic and away from paper for a while, but some people still really like checks. If you are doing business in an area where checking is popular, you will need to offer this service, which verifies the check will not bounce and leave you empty handed. The fee for this service is similar to those of a merchant account.

- Advertising and Promotion: This figure can be a little difficult to calculate unless you have given some thought to the types of advertising you want to do to launch your business and regularly promote it. As the very least, you will need to allocate funds to cover the cost of business cards, brochures, direct mail, flyers, and other types of advertising.

Transportation

Include the cost of gasoline and vehicle maintenance in your monthly estimate. This applies to whether you are a mobile detailer who will take your "shop" right to the customer or a home-based detailer who will offer pickup and drop-off service. Other costs to remember are oil changes, tune-ups, and things like windshield fluid, as well as your vehicle's monthly payment. If you keep accurate records, you can write some of this off as a business expense, but it will need to be specifically itemized on your tax return. Always record these costs immediately and keep impeccable notes.

Supplies

- *Detailing*: Carnauba wax, clay bars, paper floor mats, chamois, and even paper towels — these are all basic supplies your shop will need. There are also things like toilet paper and coffee for the coffeemaker to consider, so pick a nice round number, like $200 a month, and you will always have what you need on hand.

- *Office:* Paper, pens, folders, clips, a mousepad — all basics of the office. You won't need to replenish these quite as much, so perhaps $25 a month is fair.

- *Postage:* Earmark sufficient funds for whatever kind of mailings you plan to send each month.

What are we forgetting? There are always a few little hidden expenses in the monthly cost that you just can't predict. Magazine subscriptions for the waiting room? Dues for professional organizations? A good rule of thumb is to always keep a little money for those unexpected items.

Financing the Dream

If you can use personal savings to finance things, it's better than financing because there's no payback costs. Besides tapping in savings accounts, you may consider using other personal cash reserves such as certificates of deposit, stocks and bonds, savings bonds, and retirement funds (such as IRAs, 401(k) plans and SEPs). You can also sell real estate, jewelry, and vehicles to raise cash. Of course, if you are planning to run a large operation, taking money from outside sources may be unavoidable. Here are some financing sources you'll want to consider:

Friends & family

Yes, it's OK to ask the people close to you for money if the endeavor is sound. If you manage to convince them to back you, make sure you handle the transaction professionally. That means drawing up a promissory note for each lender that details the terms of the loan and a repayment schedule.

Sign off on paperwork and give each lender a copy. Then stick to the repayment schedule!

The last thing you want to do is sink a friendship or estrange a family member because you have broken the terms of the agreement. If you can't pay back the loan as expected, discuss the situation with honesty and the intent to find a new agreement that can facilitate that goal.

Investors

The more money you need, the more likely it will be that you need investors rather than just lenders. Just remember, investors get a percentage of your business in exchange for the backing they provide, which reduces your ownership stake. Some small-business owners turn first to friends and family to find prospective investors, but depending on the financial stake you need, you may want to look elsewhere.

Your financial institution, attorney, and/or accountant may be able to direct you to potential investors, as can the professional organizations you belong to. Sometimes, just getting the word out that you are looking for business investors is enough to generate interest. If you endeavor is sound, it will appear attractive to those looking to invest.

Fast Fact

Russia is the most dangerous country to drive in.[15]

15. **www.autoinsurance.org**, 2016.

Financial institutions

If you have a positive and long-standing relationship with a bank or credit union, you might want to make it your first stop on the road to business financing. Usually, a small community bank is more likely to agree to financing because of its commitment to the people it serves. Even so, it can be challenging to extract money from these institutions during an economic downturn.

Your local credit union is also a potential source of funding, as they tend to be a little looser than those of banks. They also offer better rates than banks overall. There is a credit union for practically every type of organization and worker, so check it out at **www.creditunionsonline.com**.

Home equity loans & lines of credit

During the great recession of the past few years, home values have typically gone down while consumer lending has tightened up considerably. This is not good news for new businesses owners. If you have a stellar credit record and a significant amount of equity, your bank or credit union may still be willing to help you. Don't give up without trying. That said, many financial institutions take a dim view of using home equity for business purposes, so be prepared for that reality.

Small Business Administration (SBA)

This government organization is the place to go if the lender you approach will not approve your loan, which sometimes happens with risky ventures. The SBA itself does not actually lend money, but it does offer a loan guarantee program that can back up to 85 percent of a small-business loan. The traditional lender works on the loan request with the nearest SBA district office, then the SBA analyzes the loan application and decides whether to back the request.

The business must be of a certain size and you must submit a boatload of paperwork to apply. The lending institution stays in the picture because it's responsible for closing the loan and ponying up the cash, then collection the payments down the road. These loans can be lifesavers for entrepreneurs but they also have higher interest rates than standard bank loans and require significantly more documentation. Plus, it can take longer to be approved since the wheels of government tend to turn more slowly.

Other options

The internet is teeming with companies who specialize in providing unsecured loans to small-business owners. Caveat alert: they often charge towering fees and have exorbitant interest rates. If you have no other choice but to go this route, investigate it thoroughly, starting with a search of its Better Business Bureau rating. Get everything in writing and have your attorney look it over so you don't miss anything that might have you on the proverbial hook forever.

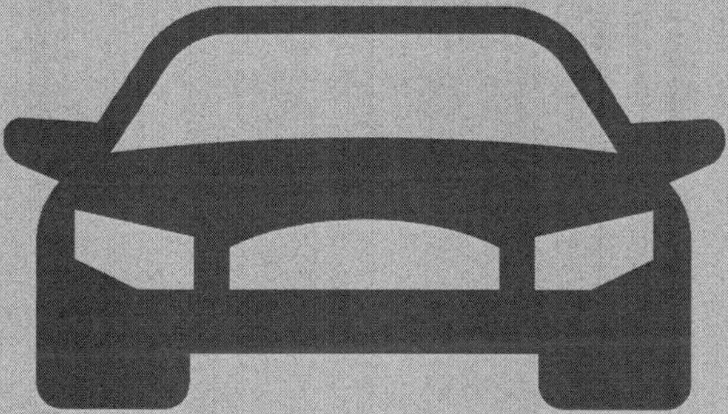

Chapter 13: Don't Run Over the Flowers

Before wrapping up this discussion on becoming a detailer, let's think about two final things that will be crucial to your success. First, environmental sustainability refers to a responsible approach you'll need to meet your current needs without harming the environment. This is particularly important for a car detailer, because many of the jobs you perform in the course of the day can have a significant impact on the earth.

From using power tools with high decibel levels to allowing contaminated soapy water to leach into the groundwater, it's up to you to promote a healthy environmental standpoint. Luckily, this is not difficult or expensive—it just takes thought. Second, you need to consider your personal enrichment. Certainly, earning a living doing something you enjoy provides plenty of that, but you can fortify yourself even more by doing things to improve your skills and keep your edge as a detailer and small business owner. Such things include pursuing educational opportunities, joining professional and allied organizations, and keeping abreast of any news that impacts the industry. Before we part ways, let's spend a little time thinking about steps you can take to be eco-friendlier and how you can stay professionally satisfied while doing it.

Protecting Mother Nature

Car detailers can be targeted by municipalities, environmental groups, and neighbors for their unwanted and sometimes noxious discharges into wastewater systems and the groundwater—and with good reason. Soaps, chemicals, and such can easily contaminate an important natural resource. For this reason, the car detailing industry has come up with various types of products and equipment to lessen this impact and make the business more sustainable.

Green products

When you wash and buff out vehicles for a living, it's easy to use a lot of water, but you can reduce that amount and still do your job well by using a waterless or dry-wash product. These products still require some water for mixing and the vehicles need to be wet. Even so, they use considerably less water.

In general, the hand wash method is estimated to use 80 to 140 gallons of water each time! To find a list of the most current products, do a quick online search using keywords. Some dry-wash products even use nonhazardous polymer resins and carnauba wax to protect the vehicle after washing can be used for buffing as well.

Eco-friendly equipment

Pressure washers are awesome, of course, but they use a lot of water. As a result, eco-conscious detailers have started using stream pressure washer to blast off dirt, rail and brake dust, road tar, and other contaminants. Certain steam machines can handle even the dirtiest vehicles, all without damaging their painted exterior, and they are compact enough to mobile detailers as well. But best of all, they have virtually no water runoff.

Fast Fact

According to Eco-Cycle, more than 100 billion pieces of junk mail are delivered in the United States each year. The production, distribution and disposal of all that junk mail creates over 51 million metric tons of greenhouses gases annually, the equivalent emissions of more than 9.3 million cars.[16]

Waste reclamation and disposal equipment

As discussed in Chapter 6, it's recommended that every mobile detailer invest in a water-reclamation system. The simplest of these systems is actually quite low-tech, consisting of a containment mat, a vacuum for captur-

16. Information hosted on **www.ecocycle.com**; garnered from a study done by Forest-Ethics in 2008.

ing greywater, and a holding tank for storing the wastewater until it can be recycled.

Of course, the idea is to keep the contaminated greywater out of the storm drains and protect the integrity of the groundwater. But containing the water is only the first step, as disposal is equally important. If greywater is only contaminated by biodegradable soap, it is usually OK to pour it into landscaped areas because plants actually appreciate the nitrogen it provides. Just be sure to switch it up and don't continually dump in the exact same spot.

The most ecologically sound thing to do is dispose of greywater in a proper sanitary sewer which is the same pipeline used to carry sewage away from the toilet. Unless you plan to dump the water into your home system, you'll have to find another arrangement. Perhaps strike a deal with the local self-serve car wash to pay a small fee to discharge water into its system.

A sanitary sewer is not to be confused with a storm sewer. The former, which you will need, takes human waste and other heavy debris away from homes and businesses. When installed, it can separate oil and other sludge before the water is released. From there, the water goes to a sewage-treatment plant to be sanitized where it can eventually return to the streams and rivers. Naturally, these nice eco-friendly systems are expensive but remember, if you don't have a proper system in place and you just put your greywater in the storm drain, the EPA will frown upon you and likely impose a paralyzing fine.

Water that goes into the storm drain is returned to rivers, streams, and lakes without any treatment and is considered blatant pollution. If you think you won't get caught, you're wrong. First, it's unconscionable to destroy the earth in such a way, and if you get caught in the crosshairs of the

EPA, you will surely need a lawyer and a whole lot of extra financing. It's not worth it.

Self-empowerment leads to success

Never stop learning. Words to live by if ever there were. Not to suggest that you should run out and get your business degree, but there are some ways to tap into ongoing learning opportunities that can expand your abilities and keep you fulfilled. You don't need to spend hundreds of dollars on a car detailing education, although that certainly isn't bad, but you can grab every chance that presents itself to learn more about your profession and your craft. Take pride in what you do and consider these options:

Regardless of whether you have been detailing for years or are just learning the ropes, ***receiving training is never wrong***. There are many trainings offered, some of which take place at certain facilities, while some are available online. There is a wide world of educational options in your field available in all different areas and at different skill levels, so head onto the wide web and check out what's going on in your area.

Even though you have chosen your career and are ready to move enthusiastically in that direction, ***signing up for a business course is brilliant***. Local community colleges have many offerings like this and can provide valuable learning opportunities for those looking to manage business more effectively. You can often just sit in on the class, not for a grade, but for the personal enrichment. You don't have to take exams or turn in work, just listen, remember, and implement what you learn. Areas like accounting, marketing, and advertising are discussed at length and will give increased confidence when facing these aspects of your own business.

Maybe you didn't know, but ***there is an association for car detailers that offers certification, education, and much more***. In addition to that, a few auto-related organizations have a detailing category among their membership ranks. Check it out online at **www.carwash.org**.

Getting involved in the community is key, and *it's helpful to take advantage of a business organization's networking and educational opportunities.* If possible, take a board member position to ramp up your visibility quotient and increase your industry connections. Even further, they often offer access to group health insurance and provide discounts and other valuable services to members

Newsletters are not just for writing; they can be quite helpful to read as well. *Industry newsletters and blogs provide tons of information and enrichment opportunities*, so pick one up or order a subscription. Jump online and enter the term "car detailing blogs" and you're off to the races!

Conclusion

Can't you just feel the road under your wheels? You're ready to take off into the sunset, my friend! You have just read everything you need to know to get started as a self-sustaining automobile detailer and small business owner. Congratulations on your decision to become a successful professional and best of luck on your path to prosperity. You can do it!

Afterword

Wow — this is an awesome book that truly explains automobile detailing. I owe my career to my love of automobile detailing and my time spent in a strong vocational education program.

I started detailing vehicles at the age of 15 working in a family's auto body and refinishing shop. I went on to three years of studying automobile refinishing at Folcroft vo-tech school in Pennsylvania.

I fell in love with automobiles, and I did quite well. My junior year, I placed second in the state of Pennsylvania VICA competition. I worked in a few shops my senior year on a work-study program and was able to meet Fred Goldman, the owner of Ardex Laboratories Inc., which is now an international detail chemical manufacturer located in Philadelphia. I worked as a route sales/service rep for four years. I met some of the nicest, dedicated people in our industry.

I left in 1984 and went into the retail automobile business, in which I also did very well, but I really missed my true love of meeting people and detailing, and Ardex gave me the opportunity to do both! So, I came back to Ardex in 1990.

I have held many positions here at Ardex through the years, and as of 2000, I am the Vice President of Sales and have continued my love of helping the future of the detailing industry worldwide through education.

If you want to get into the industry, you should get hired on at a successful private shop as an apprentice and pay very close attention to the lead detailer and the owner. Do not be afraid to start at the bottom. Sweeping floors and taking out trash is a way to show the owner that you are willing to learn the trade—make sure you *tell* them that you want to learn. Show up 10 minutes before you're supposed to, and stay a little longer than you're required to. Ask questions that won't upset other employees, and remember: a "Class A Detail Tech" is an artist! Yes, we are artists!

Practice, practice, practice! Work on your own vehicle as well as your families' vehicles. Until you're skilled and confident, you may not want to work in a volume shop (fleet or dealership) until you feel that your confidence level is high enough to compete in these spaces.

You have what it takes—put yourself out there and show everyone your artistry and business-savvy. Good luck!

P. Shawn Rowan
Vice President of Sales & Global Marketing
Ardex Labs Inc.

Appendix: The Sample Business Plan

Length and detail of this business plan: The sections of this sample business plan contain less detail than an actual business plan might need to include, depending on many variables. For instance, with many business plans, the Enterprise section might take as many as six to 11 pages, whereas in this plan it takes less than that. The product description is shortened here and fine for use, but in many business plans, up to four to eight paragraphs are needed to adequately describe product development.

Back Cover

If you have your business plan bound, which is advised, most people simply use a blank piece of card stock with no information on it. However, you can add a back cover that gives a bit more life to the business plan overall while also reminding people who you are and what your goals are. The back cover might include disclaimers or even the amount of funding you are looking for, noted once more for an investor.

(Front Cover)
Joe's Car Detailing Shop
Details Are Our Business
January 2017

Development Team:
Joe Trammell
1234 Chicago Lane
Chicago, IL 00002
Phone: 555-555-9999
Fax: 555-555-1234
website: www.joesdetailshop.com
E-mail: contactjoe@joesdetailshop.com

Executive Summary

Joe's Car Detailing Shop is an Illinois-based automobile detailing company that will clean and care for vehicles in the Chicago region. These services are available for customers with middle- to upper-level incomes. The purpose of this business plan is to outline the plans for opening and operating a car detail shop, which will be located and do business at 1234 Chicago Lane in Chicago, IL 00002, named Joe's Car Detailing Shop.

The objective of this business plan is to secure a $500,000 loan from a financial institution in order to purchase the materials needed for startup and ongoing operating costs for this business endeavor. An outline for the business's long-term marketing strategies is also included. Joe's Car Detailing Shop will be a limited liability company formed by Joe and Margarite Trammell. Joe's Car Detailing Shop is a full-service car detail shop that includes car-wash bays and more sophisticated services. Customers may pick and choose their desired detail needs, from a simple car wash to a spot-free interior and exterior treatment. Customers have the option to make an appointment, walk in, or have their car picked up from their home or place of employment for a small extra charge.

Joe's Car Detailing Shop offers customers a personal approach to having their cars cared for by a top-of-the-line detail specialist. Customers who opt to drive in can choose the level of service they would like, with choices as varied as getting fragrance, having the rims cleaned, or vacuuming the trunk. Car detail representatives are on hand to answer any questions about the products we use. We strive to make all products and our facility as eco-friendly as possible. We also offer the ability to save money the more often a customer uses Joe's Car Detailing Shop. For example, purchasing five premium details means a free premium detail the next time the customer comes in the store.

The waiting area is state- of-the-art, with television screens showing the latest movie choices and a big screen of the work being done on the car. Car items are sold in our gift shop, and products can be purchased there as well, offering customers a chance to touch up their cars in between visits. Customers may also buy gift cards for their friends and family to use at Joe's Car Detailing Shop. There are special incentives for doing so, such as more free services down the road for the gift giver. Computer screens are available in the waiting area with headphones and different channels offering customers tips and suggestions for taking the best possible care of their cars. Beyond the standard services, Joe's Car Detailing Shop also offers traditional services as noted at work or home.

A professional driver can pick up and deliver your car from your home or office for detailing service at the shop. However, Joe's Car Detailing Shop also offers a service in which we will come to your home or office and do the work on the premises. More information can be found at our website. Customers can make appointments for the at-home service either locally or even nationally, as our company is a member of the National Car Detailing Shops of America. Should you be out of town and need your car detailed, Joe's Car Detailing Shop can find a qualified and professional detailing shop in the area you are visiting.

Many shops throughout the United States are a part of the National Car Detailing Shops of America. On our website, you can either enter your ZIP code and find your own shop, or contact us through our instant-message service to have us find a detail shop for you. We will even call the shop and make the appointment for you. Customers can choose the same services they would receive at Joe's Car Detailing Shop and pay the same price as they would at our facility. If there is any problem with the service at the detail shop we recommend, customers can call our shop and discuss these problems with one of our representatives, who will take care of the problems immediately. Through our phone service, a customer can also have us make appointments with our affiliates for the dates in which the customer knows he or she will be traveling to that area.

Also at our website, customers can order from Totally Green Detailing to Save the Environment product line and have the product shipped in three working days. Customers may come into the gift shop and buy these products and others from well-known product lines. If products are not in stock, a representative will contact the customer to let him or her know as soon as stock arrives in the gift shop, or the tentatively scheduled date for shipping. Joe's Car Detailing Shop also will contact customers via email to let them know of sales and specials on products in the store or at our website. Joe's Car Detailing Shop offers services for special events in which our experienced detailers can create messages on a customer's car or truck. We use environmentally friendly products that will not damage the car's exterior. For a small fee, we will clean the car after the event as well.

Objectives

Joe's Car Detailing Shop plans to do its best to give customers a unique and personalized service from every standpoint. In the shop interacting with store associates, online, or on the telephone, we can answer any questions customers might have about our services. Customers can also take part in surveys so that we can improve our service every day, and we will encourage customers to give us suggestions about items they would like to see added to our already comprehensive list of services. Customized detailing services are our specialty, and we strive to stand out above the competition.

Services can be done in-store or at the customer's home or place of employment. Orders are accepted as customers browse our website at their leisure in their own home. Nationally, we can help customers find the right detail shop while on the road, and we will do the legwork for them if necessary. Joe's Car Detailing Shop is truly committed to making sure customers walk away satisfied and certainly with a more thorough knowledge of what is involved in the entire car detailing process and how they can benefit from this knowledge.

Mission

It is the mission of Joe's Car Detailing Shop to give every customer an excellent customer-service experience no matter how big or small the detailing job. We will offer a creative and personal approach and encourage customers to watch and understand the process of cleaning and detailing their cars. Sales associates are not only employees at Joe's Car Detailing Shop, but customer-service representatives who are dedicated to the company's overall success. They will not only be trained in doing the best detailing job possible, but will strive to know customers on a personal level, too. This, in turn, gives both the customers and the employees a unique comfort level, which is needed for customers to ask questions, thus enabling them to have a better understanding of what their car needs are now and in the future.

Keys to Success

The keys to success for Joe's Car Detailing Shop include the following:

Give customers an exceptional job and thorough understanding of the car detailing shop services and processes for their cars. Offer a continually professional and personal relationship with each customer in an effort to ensure he/she is given exceptional service and is pleased with the results of the detailing work. Cater to the customer's needs. Strive to go the extra mile to meet the customer's expectations and beyond at all times. Get to know each client on a first-name basis and remember their needs for their car as well as remembering the cars they drive while also offering any new services that are introduced in the shop. Continue to give customers an exceptional and unique experience in order to keep their business for years to come.

Statement of Purpose

Joe's Car Detailing Shop's business plan has been created to obtain money for the business in the amount of $500,000, which will be used for both startup costs and ongoing operational costs. This business plan also serves to give the potential invest or an idea in the form of an outline of Joe's Car Detailing Shop's marketing plan as well as a thorough guide to the plans for the company's future development, which could include expansion into other cities or states in the United States as well as internationally.

Company Summary

Joe's Car Detailing Shop is an Illinois-based automobile detailing company that will clean and care for vehicles in the Chicago region. Joe's Car Detailing Shop not only offers a full-service detail shop operation, but also a gift shop and a unique service in which we help our customers online and via telephone in locating a detail shop while they are traveling outside our company's region. Online services also include making appointments for pickup and delivery of the car as needed for detailing work or doing the detail job at the customer's place of employment or home.

Joe's Car Detailing Shop specializes in customer satisfaction, as every detail has been thought of with the customer's wishes in mind. Customers who visit the shop can choose from a variety of detail and car-wash products, including an eco-friendly product line patented by the company owner called Totally Green Detailing to Save the Environment. Customers who choose to have their cars picked up for service or detailed at their locations will also have as many options of buying in-shop items and/or choosing products for car detailing as those who come into the shop for detailing services.

The waiting room is a real bonus for customers, as they have the option to watch a film on a big-screen television, watch on a separate screen as their cars are detailed and serviced, or use one of several computers to get tips and information about car detailing and how to extend the life of a car's exterior and interior, whether it be leather or vinyl.

On our website, customers may order from the new Totally Green Detailing to Save the Environment product line and have the product shipped in three working days. Customers may also come into the gift shop and buy products from this line or other product lines.

Joe's Car Detailing Shop offers services for special events in which our detailers can create messages on customers' cars using environmentally friendly products. We also will clean the car after the event.

Company Ownership

Joe Trammell, owner of Joe's Car Detailing Shop, has been in the detailing and car-wash business for the past 20 years. Opening a smaller shop in

2003, Trammell legally formed the business as a sole proprietorship. Trammell graduated with a bachelor's degree in business management from the University of Texas at Austin and has always enjoyed working with cars and people. After graduation, Trammell worked in various detail shops in Texas and New York before moving to Chicago. In Chicago, he met his wife, Margarite Trammell, a chemist who played a large role in the development of his current eco-friendly product line. Together, the two patented these products and have been working on making them greener as the years have gone by and standards have changed.

Customer input and ongoing regulations have kept the products up-to-date and safe for all forms of use in the consumer and retail market. Margarite Trammell, a co-owner of Joe's Car Detailing Shop, has a degree in biology and chemistry and works on the Totally Green Detailing to Save the Environment product line. She is also working to create additional products so the detailing shop can offer an even greener form of car detailing.

Company Location and Facility

Joe's Car Detailing Shop is located at 1234 Chicago Lane, Chicago, IL 00002. Phone: 555-555-9999; website: www.joesdetailshop.com; and email: contactjoe@joesdetailshop.com.

Legal Form of Business

The legal name of the business is Joe's Car Detailing Shop, and it will operate as a sole proprietorship, as registered in the state of Illinois.

Services

Joe's Car Detailing Shop will be a full-service car detail shop including carwash bays and more sophisticated services. Customers may pick and choose their desired detail needs, from a simple car wash to a spot-free interior and exterior treatment. Customers will have the option to make an appointment, walk in, or have their car picked up from their home or place of employment for a small extra charge. Cars that are picked up are delivered back to the customer within four hours.

Joe's Car Detailing Shop offers customers a personal approach to having their car taken care of by a top-of-the-line detail specialist. Customers who drive in can choose the level of service they would like on their cars, with choices as varied as having fragrance put in the car after the service is done, having the rims cleaned on the tires, or vacuuming the trunk. Car detail representatives are on hand to answer any questions about the products we use, and we strive to make all products and our facility as eco-friendly as possible. We also offer different discount deals that give customers the ability to save money the more often they use Joe's Car Detailing Shop.

The waiting area is state-of-the-art with television screens showing the latest movie choices and a big screen of the work being done on the car, including washing, waxing, drying, and the interior cleaning process. Items for the car are also sold in our gift shop, and products can be purchased in the gift shop as well. This offers customers a chance to touch up their cars in between visits.

Customers may also buy gift cards for their friends and family. Each gift-card service bought goes toward a free detail for the customer purchasing the gift cards. Computer screens are also available in the waiting area with headphones and different channels offering customers tips and suggestions for taking the best possible care of their cars. From how to rust-proof a car to how often a car needs to be detailed for best results, these tips allow customers to make more informed decisions about the types of services and details they need.

Beyond the standard services, Joe's Car Detailing Shop also offers traditional services as noted at work or home. Of course, a professional driver can pick up and deliver a customer from his/her home or office for detailing service at the shop. However, Joe's Car Detailing Shop also offers a service in which we will come to the customer's home or office and do the work on premises. More information can be found on our website, and customers can make appointments for this at-home service either locally or even nationally, as our company is a member of the National Car Detailing Shops of America.

This means that should you be out of town and need your car detailed for whatever reason Joe's Car Detailing Shop can find a qualified and professional detailing shop in the area where you are traveling. Many shops throughout the United States are a part of the National Car Detailing Shops of America. On our website, you can either put your ZIP code in and find your own shop or contact us through our instant-message service to have us find you one. We will also call the shop and make the appointment for you. Customers can choose the same services they would receive at Joe's Car Detailing Shop and for the same price as they would pay at our facility. Both Joe's Car Detailing Shop and affiliate members of the National Car Detailing Shops of America allow services to be paid for by check, credit card, or cash. If there is any problem with the service at the detail shop we recommend, customers can call our shop and discuss these problems with one of our representatives, who will take care of it immediately.

Customers who wish to have the affiliate car detailing shop come to them while out of town can discuss this with Joe's Car Detailing Shop, and we will make the arrangements for you. Customers can pick ahead of time the services they would like to have, including a wash or a premium service. Joe's Car Detailing Shop and its affiliates also allow customers to choose the type of products they would like to have used on their vehicles. Joe's

Car Detailing Shop has a variety of products, including products from the Totally Green Detailing to Save the Environment line.

Customers can order from this new product line on our website and have the product shipped in three working days. Customers may also come in to the gift shop and buy these products or products from other lines. If products are not in stock, a representative will contact the customer to let him or her know as soon as it arrives, or the tentatively scheduled date for shipping. Joe's Car Detailing Shop will also contact customers via email to let them know of sales and specials on products in the store or at our website.

Joe's Car Detailing Shop offers services for special events in which our experienced detailers create messages on cars for weddings, parties, or even corporate functions. We use environmentally friendly products that will not damage the car's exterior. We will also, for a small fee, clean the car after the event. We recommend customized fragrances in the vehicles, and customers can choose from a variety of scents.

Market Analysis Summary

According to a survey conducted by the National Car Detailing Shops of America, the detailing and car-wash industry takes in more than $200 billion globally, and in recent years, the industry has grown 20 percent each year, with more car owners spending money on their new cars. With these numbers on the rise, operating a detailing shop providing customers the services that we have outlined make sense, as the industry is a solid investment and a major source of consumer spending.

In the Chicago area, the previous car detailing shop owned by Joe Trammell operated as the top shop offering detailing services in the area. The competition in the area does not have the luxury of a patented eco-friendly product offered to the customer, and only one other detail shop in the area actually picks up and delivers cars or comes to the customer's home or place of employment. This is truly a different type of experience for the customer, giving them a variety of options. The personal and customized attention that customers receive at Joe's Car Detail Shop is by far above the competition anywhere in the area. Also, Joe's Car Detailing will be the premier detailing shop in the area, as it provides unique services for weddings, parties, and large functions.

While Joe's Car Detailing Shop certainly caters to all ages, the bulk of the customers will be in the middle- to upper-level income bracket. The patented product line, Totally Green Detailing to Save the Environment, will certainly be a winner with all customers and even those clients who come in merely to buy the product and not have their car washed or thoroughly detailed.

Joe's Car Detailing Shop offers unique services at a price that is competitive in the Chicago area and other sources of competition online. The need for customized detailing services is a growing trend in Chicago and nationally. A large percentage of car owners living in the area who are looking to keep their cars safeguarded from the harsh winter weather without paying too much or storing their car for the winter season can use Joe's Car Detailing Shop, as we truly cater to our clientele. Owner Joe Trammell's background means professionalism, and he is known throughout the detailing world as a consummate professional.

Market Segmentation

Services at Joe's Car Detailing Shop are reasonable for any budget because of our ability to create customized packages for every customer, and the service is exceptional across the board. Pricing ranges from $25 to $150 per visit, with most customers opting to spend around $50 per visit, and the return customers keep the business going as they have their cars serviced on a biweekly basis. With detail service starting at around $25, customers can choose to simply have their car washed and dried and be on their way, still within their budget. This way, customers with a smaller budget are still able to enjoy a clean car. With the variety of services and products provided to clients, Joe's Car Detailing Shop definitely appeals to people of all ages and incomes.

Market Analysis

The market analysis of Joe's Car Detailing Shop has various market segments. With that in mind, we have broken down the customer base into four specific areas. Each section shows where the most and the least amount of profit is made for the business.

About 70 percent of the customer base with Joe's Car Detailing Shop will come from customers visiting the store and bringing their cars to us. This constitutes several services that the shop offers and, in some cases, the purchase of products to take home. This market segment is mainly made up of younger and some middle-aged men and women. The average age of customers within this segment is 33 years of age. Though many of these customers are repeat customers, promotions and advertising bring in new customers daily.

The next category is our pickup and delivery service, which constitutes about 15 percent of the customer base. These services consist of one of our professional drivers picking the car up from the customer's home or place of employment and bringing it back into the shop for the detailing work. The average age of customers within this segment is 45 years of age. This trend is due to the older executive, who does not have time to sit in the waiting room waiting for his or her car to be serviced. The customer base in this segment is made up of about 75 percent men and 25 percent women.

The trend to have the detail shop come to the home or place of employment for on-site work makes up about 7 percent of the customers. This service is simply offered to those customers who do not want to have their car driven from their location and makes up an age group from about 47 to 60, both men and women.

Eight percent of the business for Joe's Car Detail Shop will consist of online business, either product purchases or a finder's service for detail shops outside the region that our company does business with. This age group is typically across the board and consists of men and women equally.

Although the last two specific areas are certainly not the highest- grossing profit producers, they do add personality and customer- satisfaction aspects to the business overall with unique selling points.

During the past five years, Joe's Car Detailing Shop has seen a large division in the market, specifically from three different groups. These groups are quite diverse, with the largest being females ages 35 to 80. This market has a large amount of disposable income. The second group, males and females ages 20 and 45, are also interested in keeping up appearances through the use of detail-shop services. This group is, for the most part, more involved in doing things quick and easy and often will have their cars picked up and delivered to their home or place of employment.

Target Market Segment Strategy

In order to build a strong customer base, Joe's Car Detailing Shop is always interested in ways to connect on a more personally with our customers of every age and gender. While advertisement is ongoing regarding our current customer base, Joe's Car Detailing Shop is always looking for new ways to grow the customer base and support higher customer satisfaction.

A bigger customer base could provide a significant increase in sales in every area of the business simply because of the price for these services. While the competing detailing shops in the Chicago area offer some of the same services as our company, none have all the services that we offer as well as the product line.

Owner Joe Trammell has extensive experience in the world of detailing in Chicago and beyond. This, along with his wife's knowledge of the detailing business and the chemicals used in it, prove they are already major players in the detailing world.

In the next few years, Joe's Car Detailing Shop will promote special-event services, eco-friendly products, and the typical standard detailing services. The pickup and delivery service will also promote the business, as well as the at-your-service home detailing.

Promotion of detailing specials will take place on the website and the shop in Chicago, with seasonal detailing being of utmost importance, especially at winter approaches and cars need to be winterized.

Service Business Analysis

Joe's Car Detailing Shop will be a full-service car detail shop, including car-wash bays and more sophisticated services. Customers can pick and choose their desired detail needs. Customers can make an appointment, walk-in, or have their cars picked up from their home or place of employment for a small extra charge. Cars that are picked up are delivered back to the customer within four hours.

Joe's Car Detailing Shop offers customers a personal approach to having their car taken care of by top-of-the-line detail specialists. Customers who drive in can choose the level of service they would like on their cars, with choices as varied as smells in the car after the service is done, having the rims cleaned on the tires, or vacuuming the trunk. Car detail representatives are also on hand to answer any questions about the products we use, and we strive to make all products and our facility as eco-friendly as possible. Our special discount deals also offer the ability to save money the more often you use Joe's Car Detailing Shop. Special and unique services meant to cater specifically to the customer are also on our product and service menu.

Competition and Buying Patterns

In the Chicago area, the previous car detailing shop owned by Joe Trammell operated as the top shop offering detailing services. The competition in the area also does not have the luxury of a patented eco-friendly product offered to the customer, and only one other detail shop in the area actually picks up and delivers cars or comes to the customer's home or place of employment. This is truly a different type of experience for customers, giving them a variety of options. The personal and customized attention that customers receive at Joe's Car Detail Shop is by far above the competition anywhere in the area. Also, Joe's Car Detailing will be the premier detailing shop in the area, as it also provides unique services for weddings, parties, and large functions.

While Joe's Car Detailing Shop certainly caters to all ages, the bulk of the customers will be in the middle- to upper-level income bracket. The patented product line, Totally Green Detailing to Save the Environment, will certainly be a big winner with all customers and even those clients who come in to merely buy the product and not have their car washed or thoroughly detailed.

Strategy and Implementation Summary

Joe's Car Detailing Shop is always interested in ways to connect on a more personal level with customers of every age and gender in order to build a strong customer base who will use our services in the future. While advertising is ongoing regarding our current customer base, Joe's Car Detailing Shop is always looking for new ways to grow the customer base and promote higher customer satisfaction.

A bigger customer base could much improve sales in every area of the business simply because of the price for these services. Although the competing detailing shops in the Chicago area offer some of the same services as our company, none have all the services that we offer as well as the product line.

Owner Joe Trammell has extensive experience in the world of detailing in Chicago and beyond. This, along with his wife's knowledge of the detailing business and the chemicals used in it, prove they are already major players in the detailing world as well.

In the next few years, Joe's Car Detailing Shop will promote special event services and eco-friendly products, as well as the standard detailing services. The pickup and delivery service also will promote the business as will the at-your-service home detailing.

Announcements of special detailing promotions will take place at the website and shop in Chicago, with seasonal detailing being of utmost importance, especially as the winter months approach and cars need to be winterized.

Competitive Edge

It is the mission of Joe's Car Detailing Shop to give every customer an excellent customer-service experience no matter how big or small the detailing job is. We do offer a creative and personal approach and encourage customers to watch and understand the process of cleaning and detailing their cars. Sales associates are not only employees at Joe's Car Detailing Shop, but customer service representatives who are dedicated to the company's overall success. At Joe's Car Detailing Shop, customer service representatives strive to know the customers on a personal level, giving them the comfort level needed to ask questions for a better understanding of what their car needs are now and in the future. The computer tips offered on the screens in the waiting room also promote customer education, increasing the customer's overall knowledge on car detailing. This knowledge ultimately allows customers to make more informed decisions about their car detailing needs.

Back Cover

Joe's Car Detailing Shop
Details Are Our Business
Amount to Secure
$500,000
January 2017

This document is a Business Plan and is neither an offer to buy or sell as a solicitation to purchase. This Business Plan for Joe's Car Detailing Shop is confidential and includes certain proprietary information that are considered trade secrets for Joe's Car Detailing Shop. As such, neither this plan nor any of the information provided herein in this business plan may be reproduced or disclosed to any person under any circumstances without written permission of Joe's Car Detailing Shop.

Bibliography

"10 Things You Didn't Know About Cars." AutoInsurance.org. 17 Sept. 2013. Web. 14 Nov. 2016.

"7 out of 10 Consumers Use Professional Car Washes." 7 out of 10 Consumers Use Professional Car Washes. International Carwash Association, 2012. Web. 14 Nov. 2016.

"9 Fun Facts About Cars." Mr. Magic Car Wash. Mr. Magic Car Wash, 14 May 2014. Web. 14 Nov. 2016.

"Car Wash & Auto Detailing Market Research Report." Car Wash & Auto Detailing in the US Market Research. IBISWorld, Aug. 2016. Web. 14 Nov. 2016.

"Environmental Facts." *Eco-Cycle*. Eco-Cycle. Web. 14 Nov. 2016.

"National Employment." U.S. Bureau of Labor Statistics. U.S. Bureau of Labor Statistics, Sept. 2016. Web. 14 Nov. 2016.

"Who Invented the Automobile?" Who Invented the Automobile? (Everyday Mysteries: Fun Science Facts from the Library of Congress). Library of Congress. Web. 14 Nov. 2016.

Chapman University. "Survey Shows What Americans Fear Most." Science Daily. ScienceDaily, 21 October 2014. Web. 14 Nov. 2016.

Glossary

Here is a list of the common terms you might encounter as a new car detailing business owner, most of which are discussed elsewhere in this book.

Acid rain: Precipitation (including rain, snow, fog, or hail) that has combined with airborne pollutants such as sulfuric or nitric acids. It can harm a vehicle's finish and glass if not removed promptly.

Air compressor: A machine used for powering pneumatic tools.

Bonnet: Cover used on orbital buffers for the application of polishes and waxes.

Brake dust: Particles ground off the brake pads that are deposited on the braking system and wheels and can damage the wheels' finish if not removed.

Carnauba wax: A hard, yellowish-brown wax made from the leaves of the carnauba palm. The highest grade is No.1 yellow and is favored by detailers.

Carpet extractor: Device used to pull shampoo and water from carpeting after cleaning.

Chamois: Soft leather or synthetic leather-like cloth used for drying vehicles.

Claying: Process of using a clay bar to remove contaminants from painted surfaces.

Clear coat: The clear, top coat of paint applied over the pigmented layer of paint (known as the basecoat).

Creeper: Platform with wheels, on which a detailer lies in order to slide under a vehicle.

Cutting pad: Type of buffing pad for removing moderate swirls and scratches.

Demographics: Population characteristics such as age, race, gender, and income level, used to determine a target audience for marketing efforts.

Detailing clay: A product used to remove contaminants that are embedded in a vehicle's paint finish.

DBA: Acronym for "Doing Business As," referring to the name adopted by a company in place of the owner's legal name.

Dressing: Liquid (either water- or solvent-based) used to clean and shine rubber, plastic, vinyl, and leather.

Express detailing: Quickie detailing process usually completed in about 15 to 30 minutes.

Fogger odor remover: A chemical odor remover that tackles stubborn odors in or clinging to carpet, leather, vinyl, and velour.

GEM orbital polisher: Type of polisher that eliminates swirl marks. Also used to apply wax and sealants.

Gold plating: Applying a gold finish to the chrome and stainless steel of a vehicle to give it a custom, upscale look.

Headliner: The ceiling liner of a vehicle.

High-speed buffer: Device that removes scratches and other imperfections and produces high gloss and deep shine on clear coat.

Industrial fallout: Airborne metal particles that settle on a vehicle's finish, where they become embedded. Emissions from factories, as well as rail dust and brake dust, are examples of industrial fallout.

Interior dryer: Device used to speed up both interior and exterior drying.

Logotype (logo): A graphic element that identifies a company.

Merchant account: An account established with a bank or other payment processor to allow a business to accept credit-and debit-card payments.

Mission statement: A succinct statement encapsulating a business's core purpose and why it exists. Optimally it is used as a "roadmap" for future operations.

OEM: Acronym for Original Equipment Manufacturer. In the automotive industry, it refers to replacement parts manufactured by the company that made the original parts.

OSHA: Acronym for the Occupational Safety and Health Administration.

Overspray: General name for contaminants such as acid rain, fallout, brake dust, road tar, or bugs that settle on a vehicle's surface and erode the finish if not removed promptly.

Ozone generator: Device for permanently removing odors from sources such as cigarette smoke, pets, and rancid or stale food. Also kills mold, mildew, bacteria, and viruses.

Paintless dent repair (PDR): Process of removing minor dents and dings from a vehicle. Quite effective on minor body damage such as indentations and creases, door dings, and hail damage, but only if there is no paint damage.

Point of Sale (POS) terminal: Refers to the electronic box used to swipe credit/debit cards and verify that the customer's account is in good standing.

Pressure washer: Device that produces water under pressure; used for general washing and degreasing.

Rail dust: Airborne metal filings from railroads that can settle on and become embedded in a vehicle's surface. Will cause rust spots if not removed promptly

Random orbital polisher: Type of buffer used to remove scratches and scuffs. Differs from a high-speed buffer because its motion imitates hand buffing. It also is easier to master and easier to use.

Rotary buffer/polisher: High-speed buffer used to remove paint imperfections such as deep scratches and swirls.

Sand trap/oil separator: Device installed in a sanitary sewer to trap contaminants such as oil before the water is discharged into the sewer for treatment in a wastewater plant.

Skid-mount wash system: Self-contained pressure-washer unit used by mobile detailers; it can be bolted down into a truck bed or trailer.

Sustainability: A way to meet one's current needs without negatively impacting the ability of subsequent generations to meet their own needs.

Swirl marks: Micro-scratches left by wool cutting pads used on a vehicle's clear-coat finish.

Tire dressing: Solvent-based product used to condition tires.

Trade name: The official name of a business that does not use the full legal name of the owner as part of its name. Cranky Franky Auto Detailing is an example of a trade name.

Turn rate: The length of time it takes to detail a vehicle.

Wastewater-reclamation system: A system usually consisting of a containment mat that goes under the vehicle being detailed, a vacuum for collecting wastewater, and a holding tank for the water.

Wet-dry vacuum: A less powerful and less expensive alternative to a carpet extractor.

Index

About the Author

Jen Shulman is an educator and a content writer for print media. She creates published courses of study for eLearning companies, writes historical articles, and generates weekly blogs for various internet sites. Her favorite subjects are literature, history, decor, nature, and anything related to education and teaching. She holds a BA in English from UC Berkeley, a Master's Degree in Education from University of Colorado, and a secondary teaching credential in the humanities.

INTERNATIONAL DETAILING ASSOCIATION

The International Detailing Association would like to invite all detailing professionals to become members of the only independent association created for and dedicated to the true professionals of the detailing industry — **the International Detailing Association**. We believe this organization will only remain strong by helping you do the same, so IDA is constantly evolving and expanding its programs to better serve our members.

Why become a member?

▶ To be recognized as a proud IDA Member, dedicated to demonstrating your commitment to professionalism in adhering to the **IDA Code of Ethics**.

▶ To participate in the **IDA Certified Detailer Program** — the first-ever, independent, nationally recognized program of its kind! Proudly display your Certified Detailer certificate, and your Certified Detailer patch to show your customers you value professional standards enough to take this extra step.

▶ To take part in **IDA University** — educational classes, *free webinars*, and workshops dedicated to the detailing industry and held in conjunction with major regional carwash shows and conventions throughout the year.

▶ To receive the monthly **IDA e-News** with association and industry news, tips, and product updates, and participate in the social media discussion groups.

► To access the "Members Only" key features of the **IDA website** such as free webinar recordings, educational information, articles and how-to's, and business and marketing ideas to help your business grow.

► To take advantage of **business coaching** from experienced members.

IDA is dedicated to keeping your business and our industry healthy, and your participation is crucial to that effort. To join, visit our website at **www.the-ida.com/join-us**. We look forward to working with you.